CELLAR
RAT

CELLAR RAT

MY LIFE IN THE RESTAURANT UNDERBELLY

HANNAH SELINGER

Little, Brown and Company

New York   Boston   London

Little, Brown and Company
Hachette Book Group
1290 Avenue of the Americas, New York, NY 10104
littlebrown.com

First Edition: March 2025

Little, Brown and Company is a division of Hachette Book Group, Inc. The Little, Brown name and logo are trademarks of Hachette Book Group, Inc.

The publisher is not responsible for websites (or their content) that are not owned by the publisher.

The Hachette Speakers Bureau provides a wide range of authors for speaking events. To find out more, go to hachettespeakersbureau.com or email hachettespeakers@hbgusa.com.

Little, Brown and Company books may be purchased in bulk for business, educational, or promotional use. For information, please contact your local bookseller or the Hachette Book Group Special Markets Department at special.markets@hbgusa.com.

ISBN: 9780316570770
Library of Congress Control Number: 2024938288

Printing 2, 2025

LSC-C

Printed in USA

To Dan,
my straight man,
for putting up with it

To Nathaniel and Miles,
I love you more than the moon and stars

To Judith, Neil, and Rima,
for creating a writer

AUTHOR'S NOTE

This is a work of creative nonfiction. While the events are true, they may not be entirely factual. They reflect the author's recollections of experiences over time, and these memories can be flawed. Additionally, some names and identifying details have been changed, some events have been compressed, and some conversations have been reconstructed.

CELLAR
RAT

PROLOGUE

On June 29, 2020, three months into the pandemic and three days before the July 4th holiday weekend was set to begin, freelance food and wine writer Tammie Teclemariam, then best known for exposing the *Bon Appétit* editor-in-chief's 2004 brownface on Twitter, posted a thread that drew my attention. The 21-tweet post discussed a person whom I had known in a past life, Peter Meehan, the *New York Times* darling who had gone on to become the editor of the *Los Angeles Times* food section.

I first met Meehan in 2008, while I was working as the beverage director for David Chang. At the time, Meehan and Chang had been collaborating on *Momofuku: A Cookbook,* the 304-page *New York Times*–bestselling cookbook that would help launch both men into the stratosphere and set them up to take on a second literary project together, the now-defunct magazine *Lucky Peach*. The allegations against Meehan, unfolding on social media, were not entirely surprising, based on what I had personally experienced during my time at Momofuku. Teclemariam wrote of Meehan's inflated $300,000 salary, as well as reports that he sexually harassed, belittled, berated, and physically intimidated members of his staff.

"Peter Meehan has no boundaries in the workplace," she concluded. "He is unfit for real journalism."

Reading this thread sent me into an accidental tailspin. I had long since left my restaurant life behind me. I was the mother of two young children—by now just over one and three, both still in diapers—and my life was quaintly suburban. I wrote lush articles about the Hamptons' food scene for local newspapers and magazines, and national lifestyle pieces about Champagne and real estate and far-flung travel, and I thought very little about the restaurant that I had worked at 12 years earlier, when I was rounding the corner on the end of my 20s.

But something about seeing Meehan's name—first on Twitter, and then, later, in a series of news articles that chronicled the saga, which ended with him stepping down—brought me back to a place that I had not visited in a very long time. Meehan, a man who had been married with a young child when I met him, had always been a bit of an unsavory character, a little wormy. I was glad he was being held accountable for his actions but perplexed by what accountability for

Meehan meant in the broader context of the food community. Meehan was, after all, an acolyte of my former boss, David Chang, a man whom I had seen treat people terribly. I had experienced Chang's legendary wrath firsthand, and I had even tried to write about it before, but no one had been interested in that story.

Over the course of three days, I sat at my kitchen table, watching my kids through the glass sliders as they played with my husband outside. I was consumed with something that I had to get out of me, a story I couldn't keep in any longer. When I was done, I had the bones of something, the shell of a story that would become something even bigger, a story about me, and about restaurants, and about harm.

But my life in restaurants did not begin with David Chang, and it did not end with him, either. When I was finished writing 6,000 words about the Wild West of restaurant life in 2008, I realized that I had a lot more to say—both about the things that were harmful in restaurant life and also about the things that kept drawing me back, a moth to a flame. This book is the answer to some of the questions that I found in myself when I opened the door to a story in July of 2020.

Restaurants had helped me reinvent my own past. I moved to Massachusetts in 1988, my mother's home state, after living in New York for my entire life. In Massachusetts, I lived in a house that was marked by unrest: a stepfather who was, by turns, loving and abusive, ill-tempered and caring—when and if he chose to be. When my mother and stepfather split up in 1998, the year I graduated high school, I had already had a youthful lifetime full of toxicity, of looking at love through a stained-glass window. When you're taught, early on, that, in order to be loved, you have to put up with being harmed, you seek out the world's least comfortable scenarios. In restaurants I wasn't a victim; I was tough and resilient, and that made me desirable.

Keeping the truth of your emotions on the inside, of course, is not a test of strength or willpower, though; it's merely a test of your own delusion. Eventually, it just became part of my own narrative of restaurant trauma. Over time, that trauma buried itself in me so completely that I forgot the bad things about Momofuku and remembered it, instead, as a jovial, fun place to work. I did not recognize my restaurant trauma as trauma when I was going through it. It took listening to the experiences of others and understanding their stories to feel a light turn on in myself, and to recognize, in retrospect, how damaging the environments that surrounded me had been, and, moreover, how pervasive trauma can be when it is not taken seriously.

Trauma buries itself in us. A newspaper article, or a familiar name from a long time ago, could appear on a computer screen and remind us of something forceful and terrible, dragging us backward. Years later, I would hear a name and sit up in the darkness, astounded by the things I remembered. *That doesn't seem right,* I would think. *How did any of us find that acceptable?* It brought me back into a swollen, blackened worst part of myself, when work tortured me and I tortured myself in kind, running countless miles to escape something, suffering nine stress fractures in just as many years, in places like my tibia and hip bones, subsisting on 900 calories some days but still running 15 miles, sometimes before work. We were all in danger, torturing ourselves in silence. Maybe I wasn't the worst kind of addict. I wasn't doing hard drugs, and I could walk away from alcohol. But I was abusing my body in one way or another just the same, restricting calories, pounding out miles until my bones literally broke, trying to feel something on the road, over and over and over again. Restaurants are filled with people like me.

I knew, when I was at Momofuku, that this was as bad as a restaurant could get, that the language and the abuse and the treatment of staff was not normal—even though I fought to normalize it in my head. "Where would you even go from there?" a friend asked me once, when I talked about quitting or getting fired (who even knows which), and I had no real answer. But the truth is, there was no answer. To leave Momofuku was to admit failure, to concede that the game was mostly over, that I wasn't cut out for the brutality of restaurant work.

I had acknowledged, however grimly, that restaurants were unhealthy. That realization had come in stages of my emotional development in earlier places, most acutely at BLT Prime, where I worked from 2005 to 2007. But at

Momofuku, I finally understood that it wasn't sustainable. That I hung on was only a matter of survival; I had nowhere else to go. In my final months and weeks at that restaurant, I believe I knew, with some certainty, that my time was coming to an end. I was waiting, maybe, for someone to make a choice that I could not.

My time in restaurants was more than the snapshot proffered by one essay. I was, at the start, a woman naive to the charms of the restaurant world, who then became enamored of it. I became enamored of toxic culture, became a part of toxic culture, immersed by my work and unable to leave it because I felt there was nothing else out there for me. Restaurant work was fun, and magnetic, and addictive. Eventually, broken by the industry, I left, at what was probably the nadir of my personal and professional life, a time marked by both introspection and pain. And finally, I arrived at the conclusion that I could achieve success in a place that was not a restaurant, an emotional breakthrough that came with the distance of being away from restaurants, and a long-learned clarity that often only comes once we have the necessary distance from the relationships that both draw us and harm us. This book is the culmination of that journey, and the recitation of that story: a love affair, some of it unrequited. I made it out. I made it through.

It's necessary for me to point out, as I begin this book, that what I experienced in my decade of work in restaurants was through the prism of privilege. I am a white, cishet woman who grew up with financial safety nets, and when jobs evaporated—as they often did—I had support systems that could help me. My circumstances are not the same circumstances faced by the majority of restaurant workers, and I recognize my inherent advantages in telling my story. And although the experience of being a woman in my line of work was specific—particularly during the time I came up in restaurants—being a white woman and being a woman of color are not the same experience, and to omit this from the discussion would be to overlook the true depths of industry abuse. But I hope that my position as a person of privilege can help to open pathways to talking about the broader issues that plague the restaurant industry. My story is only one story. It's one story of many stories.

I also need to acknowledge that the stories in this book are true and the people in this book are real; some of them may not wish to be written about. Such is the consequence of my true and honest work. One note that I want to address here, in the prologue, is in reference to Fred Dexheimer, whom I worked under from 2005 to 2007. Fred was a mentor to me, and he became one of the youngest Master Sommeliers through the Court of Master Sommeliers when he passed the exam in 2007. In 2021, following an October 2020 accusation made public by the *New York Times*, Dexheimer had his membership revoked by the Court after an investigation concluded that he had been credibly accused of sexual harassment. During my time working for Fred, I never saw him sexually harass other women, nor was I the victim of any sexual harassment perpetrated by him. Fred's mentorship, in fact, was instrumental to my career, and I still count him as a friend and colleague. But it is necessary for me to acknowledge this reporting as I attempt to reconcile how people exist in restaurants. I am not here to diminish the stories told by others.

I also don't want to discount that many people make their careers in restaurants, and restaurant work is good, honest work. Restaurants are just one example of toxic workplace cultures that can both foster community and make extrication difficult. Restaurants are a good source of income, and they offer the promise of relative freedom. For me, the deeper I entrenched myself in restaurant life, the less free I became, and much of my diminished freedom lay at the hands of the people who employed me.

Finally, it has become necessary for me to address my relationship with my alma mater, Columbia University, a school that shaped me both as a person and as a journalist. Throughout this work, you will note references to Columbia. I am proud of the work I achieved as an undergraduate, and doubly proud of my ongoing relationship to the *Columbia Spectator*, where I worked for four years as a student journalist, and where I believe some of the country's finest reporting currently resides. As I put this book to bed, however, I bear witness to critical abuses from my university, which jeopardize free speech and which fail to recognize the humanitarian crisis currently unraveling in Gaza. I will not soon forget that my university perpetrated irreparable harm against students, when they had the opportunity to make things better, both at home and abroad.

Each chapter of this book ends with an original recipe, which is thematically linked to the chapter. I have chosen to include recipes because they are, to me, another mode of creative expression. Can a dessert be bittersweet? Can an entrée inspire nostalgia? I believe that food has the limitless capacity to inspire both emotion and conversation; if I didn't, I probably wouldn't have much of a career in the food writing world. It is my belief that my recipes, another part of my art, also have a place in this book.

This journey, of how I transformed myself from an Ivy League kid to a sommelier to persona non grata to suburban mom pecking away at the computer, is what I lay before you. I am still the cellar rat. She is still inside of me, not quite buried and bruised—but healing.

1 | PUNCH OUT

The first restaurant I ever worked in was a place called Ciro's, and it was built into a theater complex in my hometown of Newburyport, Massachusetts, population hovering around 17,000. Newburyport was once the smallest city in the Bay State (a dubious distinction that is now held by another city), framed by the rushing, thick, blue-green water of the Merrimack River—one of the most dangerous rivers in the world when it comes to boating mishaps—and notable for its brick-paved downtown that welcomes tourists in fall and summer. Picture a postcard of a New England aerial shot, complete with a white-steepled church and Colonial and Federalist buildings, and you have my hometown, bound by its allegiance to the Coast Guard (it was founded in Newburyport!) and *The Liberator* magazine (William Lloyd Garrison is also a city native).

I was born in New York City and arrived in Massachusetts

when I was 7. For a few months, we lived across the border, in a New Hampshire A-frame, while my mother and new stepfather looked for a house. I commuted to school in my new district until we bought a house built in the 1700s, the Benjamin Choate House, once a ship captain's home on a street facing the river. During a protracted phase of construction after we moved in, a machine came in and shook the foundation on the house so it leaned over to one side. If you dropped a marble in the guest room, it would slide all the way to the room's far edge. We ate dinner from a Coleman camping stove for months, and my mother built her dream kitchen: white tile floors, black glass appliances, an island made from deep-stained cherrywood.

We left that house during my sophomore year of college after my mom and stepfather split up and my mom moved across town. I had gone back to New York, to Columbia University, and my plans were to stay. You could get an apartment in the West Village for $2,000 a month back then, and some of the girls I knew did it. Williamsburg, Brooklyn, was still a shithole. If you accidentally took the N train a stop beyond Bloomingdale's, you would end up in Astoria, Queens, with its Greek restaurants and the stretch of Steinway Street known as Little Egypt, all of it still ungentrified. In "the city" (i.e., Manhattan), you could get a pack of Parliament Lights for $4, which was twice what it cost back home, on the New Hampshire border—and both felt affordable enough.

I came home to my mom's place, first for six weeks during winter break of my senior year, and then for good after graduation. It was 2002. A recession was coming, we had been told. But we had been surrounded by a blackness, a darkness, planes in our city, a tragedy around us as we, at 21, tried to figure out who we were and what we wanted to be. I came home from four years of college like a deboned fish, unprepared to move on with my life, and so I moved into the third floor of my mom's house on Ferry Road. I had vowed to get a job to stay out of my mom's hair, and so I went down to Ciro's, which was an ordinary Italian restaurant with ordinary pizzas and 30 different pasta dishes listed on a massive, laminated menu. The kitchen line ran clear from one side of the restaurant through to the next side, with a host of line cooks yelling obscenities at one another and tossing ladles of sauces into pans. The food wasn't good. The atmosphere was frenetic. But Ciro's was busy and the staff was loyal.

The Firehouse Center, the city's performance hub, sits perched at the base of Water Street and Market Square. Ciro's, the center's resident restaurant, occupied two floors, as well as a front and back patio. When the manager asked me where I had worked before, I answered, "Trattoria Pesce Pasta, in New York, but it's closed now." It was a place in the Village that I had eaten at once, in 1999, and I remembered it only because I had seen Liv Tyler there—my first Liv Tyler sighting though not my last. I wasn't convinced that the restaurant was closed, but I was fairly convinced that no one was going to check. They didn't ask for a résumé or whether or not I could open a bottle of wine, which was good, because I couldn't. I couldn't carry a tray, either, and I didn't know how to use a point-of-sale system, and I was very bad at math.

None of this seemed to matter.

I worked at Ciro's through a staggeringly hot summer, serving all kinds of mediocre marsalas to visitors who needed to grab a bite before or after a performance. I learned how to carry a tray high above my head. I wore a white shirt and black slacks and carried ballpoint pens in my pocket, and I made pretty decent cash. Some mysterious things began happening at Ciro's, though, despite how busy we were. Our wine and liquor orders began getting smaller. We started running out of things, and no one could tell us why. Although our tips were fine, our paychecks—as small as they were, given the minimum wage at the time ($2.13/hour)—started bouncing. Then, one morning in early October, I went into work to find a heavy chain and deadbolt wrapped around the door. Ciro's had gone out of business. And, just like that, I was out of my first job in the restaurant industry.

Remaining in my mother's house as an unemployed 21-year-old college graduate taking a year off to find herself was not an option, so the day that I found myself without a job at Ciro's was the same day that I walked up the street to the Grog, a tavern in a brick building with a green and white awning that had opened in the 1970s and was revered by everyone from the local day drinkers to the family set. This time, I didn't have to lie about my experience. I had made it through nearly six months of service without a major incident. I was hired on the spot.

My intention was to stay at the Grog for a few months and then move on, go to grad school, perhaps, or maybe move back to New York. But I stayed for two years, starting as a server and winding my way through the restaurant, working shifts as a cocktail waitress in the music venue in the basement known as the cabaret, and as a bartender at all three bars.

"Columbia, pick up," the chefs would call. "COLUMBIA!" It was a gentle nickname for me, the most over-educated person in there who had come back home to learn about the nuances of Alice White Chardonnay, poured out of a 1.5-liter bottle, alongside a pint of Guinness (no self-respecting Massachusetts bartender could work behind the stick without learning to pour a perfect, creamy, no-bubble Guinness, *thankyouverymuch*).

Massachusetts bar culture had a lot to teach me. At Columbia, there was no school holiday for the marauder Christopher Columbus, but all students were given an extra two days off for Election Day so that they could go home and vote. What else could you expect from the university where students once flung open the windows and established Students for a Democratic Society? (Back then, we still thought the university was liberal. Those were the days.) In Bay State bars and restaurants, though, we had other holidays to consider. Every snow day, for instance, was its own small holiday. We welcomed in the local pedestrians, who had put workdays on hold to come downtown for a pint by the fire. St. Patrick's Day was ruthlessly busy, spiraling into a green-tinged frenzy. Anytime the Patriots were playing, we could expect a line out the door. And then there were, of course, the baseball playoffs. Because no holiday could outdo the celebration when the Boston Red Sox were performing well.

Even though I spent much of my childhood in Massachusetts, I was born in New York, to a Yankees fan of a father. My first games had been at Yankee Stadium. I had waited outside of games to watch the players exit, screaming for Roberto Kelly and Paul O'Neill. In 1996, in my sophomore year of high school, my father had scored tickets to the last game of the World Series between the Atlanta Braves and the Yanks, a Game 6 matchup that had come after the Braves had led the series 2–0. Jimmy Key pitched against then-legendary Greg Maddux. We got to the stadium early enough to see Darryl Strawberry toss balls into the stands in left field. A young pitcher named Mariano Rivera was working as the setup man for a closer named John Wetteland (this was before he was indicted on child sexual assault), and reams of toilet paper erupted from the upper decks when Mark Lemke popped out to third baseman Charlie Hayes. I was a good fan. I stayed until the bitter end, cheering with everyone around me, screaming with Geraldo Rivera and

Andrew Shue, and with other strangers who loved the Yankees just as much as I did, or who hated the Braves just as much as I did. Baseball made us all feel alive.

Seven years later, in October of 2003, I had been at the Grog for one year, and the Yankees were possibly headed to the World Series again—but they had to get through the Red Sox first, in the American League Championship Series. Boston took the first game, on Yankee turf, but the Yanks came back in Game 2, with veteran starter Andy Pettitte pitching. And then there was the third game, which fell on a Saturday night, October 11.

"You can all wear your hats," my manager, Ed, told us. It was going to be a classic pitching matchup, between Pedro Martínez, the Red Sox ace, and Roger Clemens, once a Red Sox and now a Yankee. Clemens was known for his hubris and his attitude problem—his children all had names beginning with the letter K, the baseball signifier for strikeout—but he was still a powerhouse pitcher. An ornery Texan, he could turn on a dime. The hostility between New York and Boston was well-known, and players who switched between the two teams were often considered turncoats, particularly if they moved south.

A few things happened during that October 11 game. First, Karim Garcia, an outfielder for the Yankees, got beaned by Pedro Martínez, and Yankee catcher Jorge Posada exchanged words with the pitcher. The rancor then escalated. Garcia was forced out and slid into another player, one of the Red Sox charged the mound, and there was a rare bench-clearing brawl, which felled 72-year-old Yankee manager Don Zimmer and paused the game for over 13 minutes.

I had shown up for work with my Yankees hat on, taking Ed's word at face value. The mood was electric. It was baseball season. We were all excited. Every server wore a hat—a Red Sox hat. And then there was me, in my Yankees hat, in the middle of the busiest shift, Saturday night, 8 p.m., baseball playoffs.

"What is *that?*" Ed asked.

"You said I could wear a hat."

"I said you could wear a Red Sox hat."

He hadn't, of course, although I probably knew what he meant. He was smiling. I was smiling. I had no intention of removing the hat.

Technically, Ed was off his shift now. He had been on the day shift and Bill, the general manager, was on the night shift. By now, Ed had settled into his beverage of choice, a Maker's Mark and Coke, poured into a pint glass, light on the ice. He was standing a little over me, but not in a menacing way. Maybe he was swaying a little. Maybe it was his second Maker's and Coke.

"Take the hat off," he said.

"No!" I said. "Everyone else is wearing a hat. I'm going to wear a hat!"

"Take it off, or I'll punch it off your face." He was laughing now.

"Fine. Go ahead. Punch it off my face."

Ed wound back his arm to punch underneath the rim of my hat. I could see his approach and I could tell what he was trying to do. But that's when the Maker's interfered. Instead of hitting me underneath the rim of my hat, he hit me clear across the bridge of my nose. Out of instinct, I covered my face with both hands.

"Ed!" I screamed. "I think you broke my nose!"

"You're so dramatic," he said. "I did not break your nose."

I pulled my hands away from my face and my nose unleashed, as if a faucet had been turned on. Blood covered my hands. "I think I need to sit down," I said.

"Oh my god. Oh my god. Oh my god." Ed turned white as a sheet. "Get her a chair. SOMEONE GET HER A CHAIR." He ran to the back and pulled a wooden chair out near the kitchen door and motioned for me to sit down. In a minute, I was surrounded by staff. Someone took over my tables.

One of the cooks stood over me. "I think we should set it," he said. He was large and beefy and had hands the size of my forearm.

"No one is punching me in the face again!" I said. "I need to go to the hospital. I need someone to drive me to the hospital!"

My health insurance, I knew, had recently lapsed. It was the only time in my life that I had gone without insurance. I was afraid of what would happen when I got there.

"It's a work incident," Bill told me. "It's covered under workman's comp."

A cocktail waitress from the cabaret clocked out and drove me to triage, where a young doctor stuffed gauze up my nose. "There's not much we can do for a broken nose besides let it heal on its own," he said. "Don't let anything come near it while it's healing and try not to get hit in the face again. Oh, and you'll have a couple of black eyes by morning."

He was right about that.

That hospital, Anna Jaques, the hospital of my hometown, where my brother and sister had been born, sent me bills for two years. (Is it possible to feel nostalgia for a place that will happily sap you of your earnings, one hard-fought penny at a time?) They wanted payment for my still-crooked nose. I sent letter after letter, explaining that it was an accident at work. *Workers' compensation.* You can get punched in the face and they'll still send you the bill. I took each bill all the way up the creaky stairs to the tiny office on the top floor of the restaurant, where Bill and Nicole, the legacy owner of the Grog and Bill's wife, spent afternoons doing the behind-the-scenes admin. They filed my paperwork away, promising to call the hospital, but I remained in limbo, a casualty of my employers' "goodwill" and the red tape of a hospital's out-of-pocket charges. When the bills did finally stop arriving, I felt not relief, but unrest. Would a creditor arrive someday to reclaim my five-speed Volkswagen Golf, political bumper stickers and all? It was the only thing of value I owned, my ticket to freedom, a key to the open road purchased via one very large certified check for $19,200. It was the largest single payment I had ever seen in my life, a gift from my father for graduating Columbia and handed over on the last day of my city life in New York before I hit the road.

Yes, I had been punched in the face, and yes, the hospital was hunting me down, but I still loved my job. I loved the Grog. Every night after work, even after Ed broke my nose, I spent my free time at the bar.

Until I found restaurants, my life had been fairly predictable. I had been an excellent high school student who spent Saturday nights at the drive-through Dunkin' Donuts—with the exception of one epic party I threw during my senior year, which my parents never let me live down. In college, I was a consummate nerd, working nights at the college newspaper and reading 1,000 pages of 16th-century literature a week. I was supposed to go to law school after graduation, but I came home instead, to do all the fun things that everyone else had been doing when I had been reading Herodotus and Thucydides and John Locke.

The truth was, before I started working at the Grog, I had never imagined that life could be that much fun. There were no responsibilities, besides the few we had at work, and, as our reward for turning our bodies into machines for a few hours, we were given wads of cash. No one had ever really paid me much money to do anything before. In high school,

I had made $4.25 an hour working as a salesclerk at the local Hallmark store, keeping people in orderly lines when the newest shipments of Beanie Babies arrived. That had been a kid's job, with no discernible responsibility. Change the cassette tapes every once in a while, to make sure the ambient sound in the store wasn't too stale (we preferred the soundtrack to *My Best Friend's Wedding*). Operate the old cash register. Catalogue the Precious Moments figurines, each of which, valued at over $100 apiece, came with its own name and description, denoted in a hard plastic box full of index cards. Do an inventory of greeting cards that needed to be reordered. Answer the constantly ringing phones—questions, always, about those ridiculous "collectible" Beanie Babies, which, come to find out, were worth nothing at all. Contemplate lunch: McDonald's, from the far side of Port Plaza, or a bagel from the truly terrible place next door, Café Bagel, where the bagels were the size and hardness of hockey pucks. And then, of course, my favorite task: going through the Russell Stover chocolates to see which had expired. Expired boxes were ours to eat.

At the end of each workweek at Bonney's Hallmark, named for the owner, Cliff Bonney, maybe I'd walk out with a paycheck for $100, after taxes. It felt like a lot at the time, a paycheck that was entirely mine. But there wasn't much I could do with $100, not even in 1998. And so as I leaned into service—into my role as a server, and a restaurant worker—I discovered the revenue stream, too. I was young, and then there was money, much more of it than I even needed, plenty of it to help me enjoy all of the things that people who are young want to enjoy. I could eat at cheap restaurants in town, could head to Salisbury Beach for Skee-Ball and Bud Lights and wafer-thin slices of beach pizza from Cristy's—the kind with the candy-sweet sauce and the flimsy orb of provolone right in the center.

For me, the Grog was everything: It was a place to make money, a space where I could do all of the things that I had never been able to do as a goody-two-shoes academic overachiever. It was a clamorous, loud, frenetic, welcoming boardroom where anything was possible. In the soft spot that opened up between my academic foundation and my development as a person, I found that I was becoming something different: a restaurant person.

It was also an instant social stew, a place that mimicked the best parts of college, like the Heights, where my friends and I drank vodka tonics for $4 on Thursday nights. Except now, in the morning after—or, let's be honest, early afternoon—there was no tome to digest, no weight of homework, no term paper due. I was free to enjoy the camaraderie of a restaurant family without any of the baggage. After a night of service, you hang up your apron and work is finally, emphatically over. There is no mountain of work that accompanies you home. That was my parents' burden to bear, an attorney's curse, paperwork overflowing into the creases of home life.

Also, I was a fast learner. The photographic memory that had gotten me through school with ease ("You never seem to have to work very hard at it," my father had once conceded) was a help in restaurants, too. I could memorize a menu, a seating plan, the faces of guests. I didn't write down orders because I didn't need to. "Are you sure?" guests hesitated, trusting me with, they seemed to feel, their life. It was only tuxedo chicken! But I never forgot an order. I never forgot stacked orders even, tables upon tables catalogued in my brain, which had been trained to do far more than this.

I learned to carry plates three up on one arm, weathered the burns from a hot one that had sat too long under the heat lamp in the kitchen. That was my own fault, of course, for not making it back sooner to pick it up. We didn't have expeditors. We ran our own shit. On a busy night, we had to haul our asses from our sections to our computers to the kitchen and back to clear tables and then to the bar and dish pit. It was a grueling circle, a quick firing of all circuits. I zipped through the restaurant like a wind-up toy, bouncing between the service station, the bar, my five-table section, never forgetting to grab an empty plate on the way to the kitchen. My body felt activated, like it had been lit on fire. I had always had stage fright, and yet, somehow, in this one sequence of performance, I knew the choreography.

My relationship to restaurants began situationally. I needed a soft landing, or otherwise I just needed a break, and it was the right time and the right place, a confluence. It did not feel dangerous, or dark, and I did not realize, when I was accepting my first job, that I was saying yes to a career. I did not realize that something that was fun was going to be something that would become part of my life story. But this would set me on the trajectory to become a *restaurant person*. It would set my adult life in motion.

Where was I, after all, on the night that I got my letters from graduate programs—the acceptances and the rejections? I wasn't sitting at home with my parents, debating the merits of Emerson's Presidential Fellowship. I wasn't sitting around wondering why I hadn't applied to Iowa. I was out at a bar, leafing through the yeses and the noes, letting the decisions chart my life for me. I decided I'd go to Boston for two years because I'd done the narrow work of applying: only four schools—two in Boston, two in New York—and I had been accepted to half of them. I would barely have to uproot my life at all. I could come back and wait tables on the weekends, still drink with my buddies as I was writing about books and people and places. I could build a new life without leaving the old one behind. Or this was what I envisioned for myself, anyway.

For the first time in a long time, though, my life felt free, and that freedom was something I didn't want to give up. I was free to wake up in the golden light of midmorning to an empty house, without obligations. In the cool, windy fall afternoons before work, I could drive down to the beach, smoking a Parliament out of the window of my own car, drinking an iced coffee. There wasn't anyone to tell me what I could or could not do anymore, and it had never occurred to me that the rigidity of performing in academics could have a counterpoint: nothing. People did this. They just lived lives. They woke up and got coffee and drove to the beach and watched the surf froth at their feet and they went to work and they felt fine about it. They didn't feel the absolutism of accomplishment. They didn't feel like they had to do some bigger, more necessary thing. They only had to work a job that felt fun and essential to their financial survival. All of the other missing pieces were not truly missing, it turned out.

I didn't know how long I planned to stick around the Grog. I didn't want to go. I also knew, somewhere in a darkened cherry pit of me, that I couldn't really stay in my hometown forever. When I didn't feel like slinking into the third-floor bedroom at my mother's house, I crashed on friend's couches, and then, eventually, I got a condo in Boston, but no one wanted to come into the city. That felt far away from this, from the restaurant life that I loved, where we made Long Island iced teas after service and drove home measuring our sobriety against the white lines of the road. You didn't want to get caught, didn't want to see your name in the *Daily News* police roster the next day, but everyone ended up in there eventually, including me.

One by one, we all got nabbed by the cops for drinking and driving, because there isn't much else to do in a small town besides drink and then find the wrong way home.

There was only one taxi company in town and it was unreliable, particularly in the snow, and so we all tempted fate until fate bit back. One by one, we lost our licenses and showed up at arraignments and hung our heads low and hitched rides and lost our cars to impound and swore we'd learned our lessons. Some of us—not me this time—got nabbed again and again, made the papers over and over and had to dry out more than once in a cell overnight at the local police precinct. I still thought it was fun. I didn't know that some of the people I had met would die of liver failure before they hit 40. I didn't know that the word for the sadness that hung over all of us and over our industry was something we weren't brave enough to talk about. I just didn't know.

On an October night after I had worked a double shift, I drank a margarita and drove a few towns over with friends to see a band. I was technically the designated driver, and so I was supposed to be the one keeping my head above water. At the bar, I drank a Bud Light and begged off a round of shots. I remember stepping onto the curb. Was I drunk? I didn't think so. Outside, the air bit into us, prickled like it used to in October in New England, back before we knew that the earth was getting incrementally warmer, every autumn an inch closer to never really having an autumn again.

One of my friends sat in the passenger seat. "You cool?" he said. I was cool. I thought I was cool. *Cool.* It meant sober. We didn't care. It was all a lie. No one was ever fully sober. The trick was just being sober enough to get home. He snuffed out the tip of a joint—still illegal back then—and left it in the gear shift. In the back, our other friends were worse off. The car smelled like cigarettes and beer. I didn't mind. Or I couldn't smell it myself.

Heading into West Newbury, a rural town that sloped into my own, I ignored a speed trap that I had blown through a thousand times in my life. Fifty-five to thirty-five, just like that. I knew it was there. We all knew it was there, and where the cops, hungry for a late-night speeder snack, hung out in the shadows. I didn't see him pull into my lane on the darkened road, or follow, at a neat distance, to the traffic light at the top of the hill. I didn't see him follow me onto the on-ramp to Route 95 North toward Amesbury, which was when he put on his blue flashing lights.

"Shit," my friend said. "Pull over!"

But by then it was the on-ramp, at one in the morning.

"It's the on-ramp to the highway!" I said.

I waited until I was out of the way, just a quarter mile up, and pulled off on the shoulder. The highway was vacant. It was only us in the pitch-black night, a car of people who had just come from a bar and our natural enemy, a police officer.

"Do you know why I'm pulling you over?" he said, as I rolled down my window.

"I honestly don't," I said. My friend was rooting through the glove box for my registration. I held my license out.

"You were going fifty-five in a thirty-five."

The trap. What a joke. I nodded. Why lie?

"Have you been drinking?" he asked.

"I was working. At the Grog," I said. "I had a drink after my shift. That's it." It was mostly true.

"I'm going to need you to step out of the car over here."

On the side of the blank and desolate highway, the officer directed me to a line, which defined the shoulder from the rest of the road. I was to walk it, straight, heel-to-toe, one foot right in front of the other. Doing a sobriety test, even if you're dead sober, is nerve-racking. Your hands shake. You can't quite get control of your faculties. Now try doing it on the side of the highway in the middle of the night, with the knowledge that you've had two drinks on an empty stomach. I swayed. I looked to the side to see if any cars were coming. A few intermittent lights flashed by.

The officer asked me to say the alphabet backward.

"I genuinely can't do that sober," I said. I started thinking about each letter. Overthinking. After a few minutes, it was clear that I had failed.

"Step over to the side," the officer said. It felt like disappointing a parent, but worse. Much worse. "I'm going to arrest you now," he said.

My jaw dropped and then went back up again, like a fish. Whatever words I wanted to let out escaped, let out onto the highway. The officer gently backed me up and cuffed me and then placed me in the car. He radioed for backup, for a partner to drive my friends to their house in Amesbury.

"What about my car?" I asked. My prized possession, my

Volkswagen, every single detail picked out by me and then printed out and brought to the car dealership. The sunroof! The power windows! The CD player! The stupid, poorly designed cup-holder that popped out right in front of the CD player, making it impossible to drink a soda and change a CD at the same time! The armrest, which, for some reason, you had to pay extra for! I had perseverated over the details, had chosen silver and not green because silver shows less dirt. What would happen to it?

"We impound the car," the officer said. "You can pick it up tomorrow. Or the next day. But it's $150 per day at impound. You'll need to go with someone, since your license will be revoked."

I spent half the night in jail. A call to my mom went unanswered. I couldn't blame her. It was two in the morning, and she still had a landline without caller ID. But my friend Tom answered the phone and agreed to pick me up at the station. He seemed neither thrilled nor terribly surprised, but he let me crash on his couch anyway, because that's what you did when a friend got a DUI. *Dooey.* That's how you pronounced it. He tossed me a blanket. "Sober up," he said, slamming the door to his bedroom behind me.

For some, a *dooey* is a wake-up call, and for me, it kind of was. But it mostly just meant that I didn't drive when I drank anymore. I lost my license for a while, lent the Volkswagen to a friend, and hitched rides if I planned on drinking, which was still often enough. To shake off any sense that life was spinning like a sideways top, I sang karaoke on Mondays and a cappella on Wednesdays at open-mic night—Hoot Night, they called it—since I didn't know how to play the guitar. I had a paralyzing fear of public speaking, but something about the crowd made me want to jump in headfirst.

I had an idea about leaving, about heading off to graduate school and writing the Great American Novel and not working in restaurants any longer, but I was equally paralyzed by fear. In a very short period of time, I had been punched in the face and arrested. My name had appeared in the local newspaper for *speeding* and *failing to stop for a police officer* and *possession of a controlled substance*—that was the stubbed end of that joint that hadn't belonged to me that had made its way into the gear shift—and *driving under the influence of alcohol.* I had gotten calls from people I had gone to high school with. Had I gone on a high-speed chase through town with drugs in the car, they wanted to know? Good ole COLUMBIA had certainly fallen from grace.

Shaking off the dust from restaurants was hard, though. Separating myself was like stripping sinew from bone. I felt like a surgeon, making small cuts on a daily basis. Winnowing myself down, remembering why I moved home, thinking back to the person I had been before planes had crashed into buildings, thinking back to all the potential that I had when I was 18 and had left for New York. I was an empty vessel back then, hoping to be filled up with knowledge, with good deeds, with possibility. You can't go back to those earlier days, but you can find a landing somewhere in between. That was what I needed: a safe landing.

My nose started to heal. Black eyes became black circles and soon I couldn't see anything at all beneath the pale, thin skin. The bridge of my nose would always betray the blow lent to it, a tiny notch as proof of old pain, an old wound. The body heals, and it also hides and stores trauma, every former ache, a history of damages done. My license restored, I was free once more to move about Massachusetts, to draw a larger and larger circle, expanding like an ever-widening hula hoop. I wanted a bigger life. I wanted to move on.

The romantic in me, though, still sidled up to the bar on an occasional night back in town. I'd order a Bud Light, extra cold. Mostly, the bar would stay the same, even as I didn't. The passage of time was suspended in bars, or just this bar. People didn't leave. I was a former employee, and then I was just another regular, treated with the requisite dignity: cold beer, occasional drink on the house. After a while, I was just an anonymous person at an anonymous bar, and no one but me remembered the story about getting punched in the face, and it was mine to stow away, under the lock and key of memory.

*　　*　　*

Bourbon and Coke Bundt Cake

Serves 12 to 16

CAKE

24 tablespoons (1½ cups; 375 grams) unsalted butter, softened, plus more for the pan

½ cup (62.5 grams) unsweetened cocoa powder, sifted, plus more for the pan

2½ cups (500 grams) granulated sugar

3 large eggs, at room temperature

1½ teaspoons vanilla extract

3 cups (360 grams) all-purpose flour

1½ teaspoons baking soda

½ teaspoon table salt

1 cup (240 grams) Coca-Cola, preferably Mexican Coke if available

¾ cup (177 grams) full-fat buttermilk

½ cup (118 grams) bourbon

GLAZE

4 tablespoons (62.5 grams) salted butter

3 tablespoons Coca-Cola, or as needed

2 tablespoons plus 1½ teaspoons unsweetened cocoa powder

1 tablespoon bourbon

2 cups plus 2 tablespoons (265.62 grams) confectioners' sugar, or as needed

For the cake: Preheat the oven to 350°F. Generously grease a 12-cup Bundt pan with butter, then coat liberally with cocoa powder, shaking out any excess.

Place the 24 tablespoons butter in the bowl of a stand mixer fitted with a paddle attachment or use a handheld electric mixer. Beat on medium speed for several minutes, until lightened and creamy. Stop to scrape down the bowl.

Gradually add the granulated sugar, beating on medium speed until well incorporated. Reduce the speed to low and add the eggs one at a time, beating to incorporate after each addition, then beat in the vanilla. Stop to scrape down the bowl.

Whisk together the flour, ½ cup cocoa powder, baking soda, and salt in a medium bowl. Stir together the Coke, buttermilk, and bourbon in a large liquid measuring cup.

Beating on low speed, add the flour mixture alternately with the Coke mixture to the batter until just combined, beginning and ending with the flour mixture and stopping to scrape down the bowl as needed. The batter will be thick, creamy, and smooth. Transfer to your prepared pan, spreading it evenly.

Bake (middle rack) for 40 to 45 minutes, until a tester inserted into the thickest part of the cake comes out clean. Cool in the pan on a wire rack for 10 minutes, then carefully invert and dislodge the cake from the pan onto the rack and cool for 30 minutes.

For the glaze: Combine the butter, Coke, and cocoa powder in a small saucepan over medium-low heat, stirring until the butter melts. Remove from the heat and stir in the bourbon.

Sift the confectioners' sugar into a mixing bowl. Add the bourbon mixture, then use a sturdy whisk or a handheld electric mixer (medium speed) to beat until the consistency of an icing. Thicken with more confectioners' sugar (adding a tablespoon at a time) or thin with more Coke, as needed. Let the warm glaze rest for a minute or two (to settle any bubbles) before drizzling over the cake.

Serve once the glaze has set.

2 | BAR AMERICAIN

wanted to write the next Great American Novel. In my senior year of college, I spent tortuous hours fashioning the language of short stories. I was taking a drawing class at the same time, and our final project focused on pairing words with images. A short story I had written about a crack in the ceiling of a New York City apartment—it was really about the dissolution of a marriage, which I both knew something about and also knew almost nothing about—was the baseline for a collection of amateur pen-and-ink pieces of artwork that I had bound like a book. The art was a B+ effort, my professor thought, but the story was good. Jhumpa Lahiri, my Pulitzer Prize–winning creative writing instructor, commended my talent. I could make myself small, fit into the minds of people who looked and sounded nothing like me, the key to the artistry of fiction. She believed something about me that I didn't yet believe about myself.

I secretly believed that the architecture of fiction didn't suit me at all. I was always a truth teller, always looking for the kernel of the story that said something about me and not about the world. If my characters were male or married or from some far-flung state, that was only an abstraction. Really, they were just another version of me: me in another place or me in another state of being. I didn't know then that it wasn't a complex, robust Great American Novel I was writing, but instead a flattened-out version of my own story, one that I couldn't possibly have fully developed at age 22. I didn't have the imagination necessary to conjure from thin air a Rabbit Angstrom, a Frank Bascombe, a Macon Leary. I was good, and I definitely was not yet great.

I didn't know any of these things about myself when I finished graduate school in Boston in 2005. Committed, still, to the idea of writing and selling a book and becoming the kind of writer with a foothold in the most elite literary circles, I left Boston for New York again, determined to find a home for myself in editorial. A recession had hit a few years before, and jobs were hard to come by. The average starting pay for an editorial assistant in publishing was a little over $25,000 per year, about 52 percent of the annual rent of the slightly-cockroach-infested-but-still-imbued-with-lovely-pre-war-details one-bedroom apartment I found in Astoria. The apartment faced an airshaft, had a galley kitchen, and anytime I used an air conditioner and hair dryer at the same time, it blew an old glass fuse, which was located, rather inconveniently, six feet up in the entryway, meaning fumbling around in the dark for a chair to replace it. But it was, in those early days that I dreamed of being the kind of writer who wrote a book, an apartment that was mine and only mine, and so I ignored the roach bodies that turned to dust in the backs of closets and cupboards, and called 1-800-Mattress when I discovered a bedbug infestation and needed the nightmare remedied immediately, and, yes, learned to change fuses in the pitch dark.

I got a job that I first thought of as a temporary job but that I eventually started to think of as an actual job, which is what happens when you are living in New York and are faced with an onslaught of bills. My work in the service industry had been completely unpolished back in Massachusetts, and I had known better than to expect that I could walk into a restaurant in New York without serious experience and pedigree and snag a job. Still, it was an era before the wide use of Craigslist, before widespread Internet searches, and before names appeared on Google hit lists. My father suggested searching the *New York Times* for job listings, which is how I stumbled upon an open call for restaurant work at a place that had just opened on West 52nd Street, a glossy, vibey space from celebrity chef Bobby Flay.

Bar Americain was a high-ceilinged bistro that opened in 2005 and thrived with Theater District verve. Once Judson Grill, another spot that had drawn large crowds, the space had been transformed into a different large dining room, seating 200. To hear Frank Bruni tell it in his two-star review of the restaurant for the *Times* in June of 2005, Bar Americain was pleasurable. "Simply put," he wrote, "it's fun." Bruni focused on the restaurant's orange-hued interior, a glowing, throbbing luminescence. It did have a warm and happy feel, Art Deco accents, and sunny lighting, thanks to the conceptual design firm the Rockwell Group.

The restaurant also had servers in bistro-chic waist aprons. Restaurant partner Laurence Kretchmer, ruthlessly handsome and thin, arrived frequently, happy to parade around the restaurant in an expensive suit. It was his job to make guests feel a little bit important, flexing his own muscles and theirs. Bar Americain was a place to see and be seen, even though it resided fully in an uncool part of New York, unpleasantly close to Times Square, even more unpleasantly close to the section of the city where diners needed to be finished with dinner before showtime (let's call it what it is: the 6 p.m. reservation). It wasn't an occasion restaurant so much as a convenient stopover for those in need of a burnished place to post up at after work or before a performance. But that position alone made it extremely busy, extremely popular, and extremely profitable.

I was completely unequipped to work at this restaurant, which required New York City experience. Did I have New York City experience, a slick French manager, the name of whom escapes me now, wanted to know.

"Of course," I said, producing a résumé with many truths and one abject untruth. On it, I had added the name of a restaurant I was not sure even existed, a place in the Village that I dined at in college. "I worked at a few places in my hometown—here are my references," I said. "I also worked at Trattoria Pesce Pasta," I added, hoping the New York network of who-knows-who wouldn't come back to bite me in the ass.

"When can you start?" he wanted to know.

In my head, I did the math. There was the Astoria rent, the Sprint bill for my flip phone, the cash necessary to replenish my MetroCard. I'd have to eat, of course. My Con Edison bill was $43 per month. I could use a paycheck sooner rather than later.

"Immediately. As soon as you need me," I said.

After being hired on the spot at Bar Americain, I had to learn how to be a fine dining server in five days. That's the amount of time a server gets in a training rotation, following around a senior server, memorizing the floor plan, learning the cadence, learning the rules, learning a new computer system. I had never worked in a proper fine dining restaurant before, so learning to serve, in any real capacity, was like learning a foreign language. At the Grog, I had rarely pulled out a waiter's pad to write down orders, committing nearly everything to memory. But at Bar Americain, entire orders were taken at once: appetizers, assigned to guests by position numbers in the computer, followed by a course line and then entrées. The kitchen's expeditor would then know which food went to which person by the signifier offered through the server's code in the computer. To make this even more confusing, female diners were distinguished with an "L"—an archaic reference to "ladies"—through order codes, because, in fine dining, women were always served first.

Each table in the dining room had, then, not just a number, but also a set of seat numbers: position one, position two, position three, position four. Adding an order to a computer might look something like this:

Blue Cheese Chips	ALL
Half Doz Oysters	L1
Tuna Tartare	2
Shrimp Cocktail	L3
Grits with Gulf Shrimp	4
Hanger Steak RARE	L1
Skate	2
Lamb MED RARE	L3
Pork Rack MED	4
Creamed Corn	ALL
Squash Blossoms	ALL

This information would be added all at once, in order, so that the kitchen would have on hand the table's first two courses. After appetizers had dropped, I would circle back to the computer—or, if time failed me, to the kitchen—and fire the entrées. Computer systems had a button for this express purpose. *Fire,* the button read, and a red alert would transmit back to the kitchen, letting them know to start working on the next course. Once the appetizer plates were removed, there was an additional step on my end, too. Mise-en-place, meaning "everything in its place," was my endless job of keeping up with appropriate silverware. Did the guest have a steak knife for a soon-to-arrive lamb course? Had the area been cleaned—or "crumbed," as we called it—before the plates hit the tablecloth? Each step in the line of progression was essential before the next. Each step was easy to remember when you only had one table and easy to forget when you found yourself in a fully sat section of five or six.

If I felt sure in my footing as a server at mediocre casual restaurants, that certainty did not translate to this world where mounting tasks and responsibilities changed the geography of the dining room. A flamboyant server who went by Boo was better, faster, and more sure-footed than I was, which is why he was assigned the bigger and better-paying sections. Unlike most of the city's great restaurants, Bar Americain was not a pooled house. Each server cashed out tips at the end of the night and kept what was brought in from that specific section, so when Boo took over section 1—all massive round tables full of heavy drinkers, desirable for the large tabs they amassed—it was no surprise that he left with wads of cash, bills to be spent at Park Bar on 15th, where the crew headed after work.

"Girl, you need to learn how to carry a *tray*," he said as he walked swiftly and meaningfully past me. One martini was fine on a bar tray, but four I definitely could not handle. Boo could, and did, marching through a busy floor without missing a step. He had the kind of personality that made people leave large tips and dumb smiley faces and notes that said *Excellent service!!!* at the bottom of the bill. I had the kind of demeanor that projected a dry throat and terror. My guests must have known how much I did not want to be there, how eager I was for the clock to charge through its seconds, minutes, hours, until the end of the shift.

A few kind work companions did take me under their wings. There was Bill, a bartender who had worked for Bobby Flay for a few years, first at the celebrity chef's Gramercy outpost, Mesa Grill. In a bow tie and vest, Bill cracked the same joke tirelessly. It was summer, we were hot, we needed relief. "Welcome to my ool. Notice there's no P in it," he said, and we cackled like it was the funniest thing we'd ever heard, because we were busy, and because when you're busy on the floor, a short and shameless joke is the only human connection you have time for. There was Ryan, too, a recovering alcoholic who lived in Brooklyn and styled his hair in a pompadour. He hadn't been sober for long enough to make good or great decisions, but he was kind and seemed to want to exceed the expectations of the industry.

Mostly, though, Bar Americain was eat or be eaten. Work was a thick cloud, tiny silver trays topped with white serviettes where silverware lived for mise-en-place; a raw bar of pebbled ice and foreign seafood treasures; floor-to-ceiling EuroCaves full of wine whose labels might as well have been written in hieroglyphs. Our sommelier, Adam, was meant to attend to guests with wine-related questions, but sometimes he couldn't get to a table in time. One night, I just got unlucky.

"I'll have this white Burgundy," the man said, pointing to a bottle on the list that I couldn't see. I wasn't looking at the name of the wine, necessarily. Instead, I was processing conflicting information that resided deep within myself. *How could something be both burgundy and white at the same time?*

"Oh," I said.

"I can tell you're confused," he said.

"It's just..." I said, without finishing.

"You're wondering how a Burgundy can be white," he said.

"Yes, that's definitely it," I said.

"It's a region," the man said. "Burgundy is a region. In France. White Burgundy refers to white wine from the Burgundy region." My face turned red. Burgundy, even. Not knowing made me feel like a rube. The man ordering the wine was being generous. He was older, possibly from the Upper West Side. He hadn't been trying to embarrass me. The extension of knowledge, as he saw it—I think, at least—was an attempt to help me, to steady me in a place where I was so obviously unsteady.

I still held the bottles of wine close to my heart when opening them, despite all the times that people at Ciro's and the Grog had told me not to, despite the warnings that had turned into tragedy, thanks to a bottle of red exploding onto a white work shirt. I knew better, sure, but, also, I didn't, because opening a bottle with a waiter's corkscrew was still terribly difficult in unpracticed hands, because no one had taught me how to hack it, because in my years waiting tables in shittier restaurants, people had—let's be honest here—mostly ordered Bud Lights and the occasional Grand Marnier margarita or a Grateful Dead, never a *white Burgundy*. For all my education and fancy family vacations, I had never once noticed that a proper waiter's tool, tucked into an apron in a nicer restaurant, has not one delicate arm, but two, an extra hinge to wrest the cork from the neck.

Knowing this trick would have saved me a little anguish, I guess. I would have known that opening a bottle of wine is not just showmanship, or mastery; it's simply hacking the game. There is a reason, after all, that a single-pull wine key is likely to snap a cork in two, or splash liquid all over a starched shirt. That type of device requires more pressure—a tabletop, a firm surface. If you happen to be opening your bottle in midair, beside a guest, you need the correct tool, and I did not have anything even close.

The real lesson, though, was about my naivete. My general lack of knowledge. My greenness. I was fresh, new, raw, and not good at my job, and I wasn't sure whether that meant that I could never be good at it or that I could someday be very good at it. The geography of wine felt boundless. I watched Adam enter and exit the wine room with mysterious bottles with mysterious names, labels I couldn't pronounce from regions of the world I couldn't find on a map. Even in my father's home, where wine lived in a small, temperature-controlled fridge and was charted on a notepad in a series of data points—drink, do not drink, good now, good in 10 years, good in 15 years, good in 20 years—I couldn't get past the obscurity. Wine felt oppositional, intellect over sensation. How were you supposed to apply reasoning to sense memory? How were you supposed to impart your perspective of the world onto the contents of the glass? Surely it wasn't that easy, to read Robert Parker's tome about Bordeaux and suddenly understand the distinction of grapes grown on one bank or another of a random French river. I did not believe that I could ever be good at understanding, appreciating, or loving a world obsessed with phrases like *sweaty saddle* and *Brettanomyces* and *pencil shavings,* because, in a nutshell, it all felt really full of shit.

By 2005, Jeffrey Steingarten had already written his two famous books on food: *The Man Who Ate Everything* and *It Must've Been Something I Ate.* Along with Ed Levine, founder of the website Serious Eats, Steingarten hosted a show called *New York Eats* on the Metro channel, diving headfirst into the city's most important food. But I didn't know Steingarten. In the late 1990s and early 2000s, culinary heroes were known mostly by name and not by face. In the emerging Internet era, restaurant anonymity was still possible. Steingarten would go on to polish his bombastic and slightly ornery personality on television, appearing as a judge on *Iron Chef,* but when he came in to dine at Bar Americain, the show was only just reaching an American audience. In an era that predated media saturation, it was still possible to see a rotund, gray-haired diner at a table as just another person eating lunch.

He ordered the Kentucky hot brown, an open-faced sandwich with turkey, bacon, and Mornay sauce. With his napkin tucked into his business shirt, he looked more like an oversize child, sunken into a banquette, than a prominent food writer. Either way, I didn't recognize him, and the maître d' didn't either, which is why I had received no soignée, a piece of paper denoting a person's VIP status. Food writers get them. All members of the media. Celebrities, big and small. Restaurant investors. A soignée for Steingarten never appeared, and so when he asked whether our ice cream was made in house, I had to rush into the kitchen to ask. I can say now, with some certainty, that no fine dining restaurant would outsource the relatively simple work of making ice cream. It's just a base of crème anglaise with flavoring that is tossed into a Pacojet, a machine that almost every expensive kitchen has—and this kitchen was very expensive.

"What are the flavors?" Steingarten needed to know. That sent me racing back into the kitchen a second time, searching for the pastry chef.

"You don't know the ice cream flavors?" the chef barked. "What kind of fucking idiot are you?" (Answer: the kind of fucking idiot who also did not know that the ice cream was made here, and not somewhere else, but anyway.)

Back at the table, Steingarten naturally had more questions. Did the vanilla come from Madagascar? (Jesus fucking Christ.) Were the strawberries local and seasonal, or were they sourced from somewhere else, like California? (Dear god, please do not make me go back and talk to the pastry chef again.) And, also, what flavor did I recommend? (As if I had tried any of these godforsaken ice creams.) Pleasing a food writer may be an impossible task, but I was also incompetent. I was untrained. I was ruthlessly bad at working in restaurants, not just from a technical standpoint—could I carry a tray competently? no, I could not—but also from a subjective standpoint. The language of food and wine was so complex and so foreign to me that I did not even know what I didn't know. Until Steingarten brought up the notion of Madagascar vanilla, I'm not sure it had even occurred to me that a distinction existed. I paused there, in the dining room, for a second, thinking about just that, about the provenance of ingredients, about how I had been eating things for many years without thinking much about where they had come from or even about their variation, about how my mother had always stuck her hands in the warm dirt, over and over again each spring and summer, soaking in the pleasure of her garden, and yet I had thought little of the differences in the varieties of individual tomatoes. Or vanilla. Or any agricultural product, really.

When I had thought about food and about cooking before, it had been such a cursory love. I had been fascinated, always, with gourmet grocery stores and ingredients that I had never seen before. But I had never thought—not on any real level—about the things that were right in front of me, the complexities of fruits and vegetables, the lineage of food, the never-ending parade of where things came from. New York, a city of industry, seemed like an unlikely place to come to a stuttering realization about the broadness of food. Still, here I was, in a Rockwell Group dining room, thinking about how Madagascar vanilla beans, grown as pods on the orchid plant *Vanilla planifolia*—OK, it was an abstraction to me then, but I was beginning to know a seedling—grew on a hot, humid island in the middle of the Indian Ocean and tasted different, more fragrant, more like vanilla, than the vanilla in any scoop of Breyers ice cream sold in a cheap black plastic container in a Massachusetts Market Basket. I was thinking about the tiers of food, about its layers and about how far something could travel and about how hard-earned flavor could be. So many of those thoughts, for me, had been conceptual, perhaps, but not really applicable, or not until I had been faced with the weight of ice cream, because as much as the expedition back and forth annoyed me, it also spurred in me a new notion of what food meant, of its inherent possibility.

In Massachusetts, we have Woodman's of Essex, the clam shack opened by Lawrence "Chubby" Woodman in 1914. Known for his famous fried potato chips, Woodman invented the fried clam at the suggestion of a friend, battering and crisping the local bivalves and selling them hot by the side of the road. Fried clams later became a local sensation, beloved by denizens of and visitors to the North Shore alike. I knew fried belly clams, fat and juicy, bursting with the ocean, stretchy at the neck. Where I came from, we rarely ate oysters. Wellfleets came north every once in a while. Littleneck and soft-shell clams—also known as steamers, the kind used for frying—were the most popular shellfish, second only to lobster. The elegance and metropolitan charm of the raw bar remained, to me at least, a relative mystery. I hadn't yet found the joy in the slippery drip of an oyster. A whelk? Despite my summers in camp in Maine, where we often found ourselves at the frigid shoreline, I didn't know what it was or how to eat it. When guests divined from the shell a twisted muscle of meat, I turned away, secretly disgusted.

I should have been tending to a busy section on the night that Bobby Flay taught me about the raw bar. It spanned the width of nearly the whole restaurant, a set piece at the back, where guests could watch practiced shuckers pick through shell after shell, flipping coins of meat, turning over those slippery, wet discs, dozen after dozen. Bobby didn't find himself in the kitchen much anymore. He had recently been tapped to perform on *Iron Chef America,* following a stint of successful Food Network shows, and he had recently married Stephanie March, a tall, beautiful, blond actress who played Alexandra Cabot—a kind but no-nonsense assistant district attorney—on *Law & Order: Special Victims Unit.* Bobby liked to come in, sure, put on his chef's whites and tool around the restaurant for the glory of it, like back in the Mesa Grill and Bolo days, but he wasn't really a *chef* as much as he was a *personality,* allowing the public exactly what they wanted: a glimpse into the momentum and power fueling the New York restaurant industry.

For whatever reason, on that particular busy night, he saw in that lost dog version of me a palpable project.

"What's your name?" he asked, grabbing me by the elbow. I was standing by the service station nearest the raw bar, probably staring too long at my notepad.

I told him.

"How long have you worked here?"

It hadn't been long. Only a few weeks.

He held up two different oysters.

"Do you know what these are?" he wanted to know.

"Oysters?" I said, voice lilting into a question mark. I knew they were oysters. Of course, I knew they were oysters.

"Is that a question?"

"Oysters," I repeated, more declaratively.

"Oysters, but where are they from?"

That part I couldn't be sure of.

"Come over here," he said. He tapped the metal bar in front of him, where oysters were being shucked. Fragments of shell and wet towels covered the surface. "Come look at these oysters." I tucked my body behind the line. To work behind the line, you have to erase yourself. You have to learn to be smaller, to fold yourself in half. This is true, indeed, of all restaurant work: to learn to exist in a way that is meaningful to other people, you have to make yourself incredibly small. There is no other way to fit. Bobby Flay grabbed one of my hands. "Hold on," he said.

In my outstretched palm, he placed a small oyster, from the West Coast. "This is a Kumamoto," he said. "See how small it is?" The oyster was, indeed, very small, half the size of the oysters I was used to seeing. It had a ruffled texture on the exterior of the shell and a deep, notched pit in the center. "Wait, let me open it." Taking the oyster back, he laid the bivalve flat upon a white and blue towel, wedging a flat knife between the joint. The oyster showed no sign of argument, splayed open to reveal an iridescent interior shell, along with a slate orb of meat. Bobby flipped the knife underneath the connective tissue, releasing the meat in one quick motion. "Here," he said, raising the shell to my mouth. "Cucumber and melon."

Once he said it, I could taste it, the roundness of the oyster, the faint line of melon, a prickle at first and then rising to a crescendo. The only oysters I had ever tasted had been saline, briny, and a little bit slimy. I had eaten an oyster as a shooter in San Francisco, and it had been OK, but this oyster—clean, with the faintest reminder of fresh-cut lawn—tasted different. I looked at him, a little puzzled.

"It's very good, right?"

It was.

Next, Bobby motioned to the chef on the raw station to hand him a prep container full of whelks. The spiraled sea snails were much larger than anything used in escargot dishes, much larger than anything seen on a rock at a familiar lake or beach. "Have you eaten a whelk?" he asked, already knowing, I suspected, the answer.

I shook my head.

He wedged a cocktail fork into the cold shell, piercing the meat and then twisting once, hard. The whelk came out in one smooth, pink piece. "That's it," he said, handing the fork to me. "That's all there is to it." The station was full of sauces—cocktail mixes and mignonettes and lemon wedges—but Bobby suggested none of it. He wanted me to eat the foods as they appeared when you first found them, naked, souls bared. A whelk, he wanted me to know, was supposed to taste like the ocean. Teased from the shell, it was chewy, briny, far more aggressive than the oyster had been. But I could see the appeal.

"Now you know the difference," he said. Whelk, oyster. West and East Coasts, competing in his rough, kitchen-weathered hand. Standing at the back of the restaurant, I could see what he saw, night after night, the entire room, the buzz, the servers moving like ants, the warm orange lights that Bruni seemed to have such fondness for, the clink of glasses, the hum of service. The middle of a rush has an electricity, and that electricity works its way into the fibers of every single person in the restaurant, from the people on the floor to the people in the seats to the people behind the line. I stood there for what felt like a very long time, but it was probably only a minute or two. I had to get back to those tables, the ones who needed martinis and Gibsons and their own plates of ice-cold oysters and whelks.

Bobby had moved on, anyway, fascinated now by some other intricacy of the dining room. Perhaps he wanted to know why a plate had been sent back, or else he was making a round in the room, the typical performance of a now-celebrity chef. *How is everything here tonight?* The peals of delight. The recognition. *Oh, is that...Yes, it's him. He still works the dining room, even with all his television fame.*

The dining room felt powerful, and working at Bar Americain, in 2005, felt powerful too. When I filled out my application, just by chance, I had no idea that I was entering a world that would challenge my notions of what it meant to dine. Not to eat. To *dine*. On occasion, I had eaten at nice restaurants, with cheese carts, and dishes that were too complex for me to understand. But I had never fully immersed myself in the spaces that carried the language and passion of that kind of dining. In fact, it had never occurred to me that there were career waiters who spent their lives perfecting the craft of service—that it meant something to be hospitable, to learn the rules of what to do in a restaurant. It had never once crossed my mind that studying the art of service was as essential to fine dining as studying literature had been to my degree in English. How else could a server arrive seamlessly at a table, set the stage for future courses, know which glassware to present, which silverware to bring, remove plates before the next dutifully arrived, and turn the table in under two hours, all without a guest feeling a single prick of anxiety? This movement through the course of service was, I would learn, a practiced, honed skill, like any other skill.

It felt expansive to work at this place, to know these people, to be immersed in this shiny, important culture. After service, team members left through an entrance at the rear of the restaurant. Unlike back home at the Grog, we were not permitted to walk through the restaurant in our normal clothes—our "street clothes," as they were called. If we wanted to come in to dine, we needed to make a reservation through the maître d', where we would receive an employee discount. Otherwise, we could join the ranks of everyone else in Midtown at the bar, bodies pressed several deep and shouting above the din. *Excuse me. Excuse me! Sir!*

It felt diminishing, too. Every time I felt confident enough to display my newly shined skills in the dining room, something would go terribly wrong. A table ordered martinis—dreaded martinis. I had been given prime real estate, a section of five tables, one of which boasted a round, perfect six-top. When one table starts an order with an impossible-to-carry drink, the law of service states that the others must follow in chorus. It's the power of suggestion. Doesn't a cold martini sound good? You can almost taste it in the glass, the olive bouncing around, the tinge of fire from the alcohol, maybe a swipe of sweet from the vermouth (or, who knows, maybe you prefer yours so dry that it's just a whisper). If the first guest at a table orders a martini—if the first guest at a very large table orders a martini: sudden and certain doom.

"I'll have a martini," the man in the business suit said.

"A martini!" a second guest chimed in. "That sounds so good!"

"Martini! Martini!" It rose like a chant.

"Let's make it a round!"

The only thing worse than carrying a martini across the floor of a busy dining room is seeing the expression of the bartender when you've rung in six martinis during a busy bar service. A proper bar shaker holds, say, two ice-cold martinis. Also, no matter how many times a bar manager stocks up, martini glasses are always in short supply. With their delicate stems and wide, triangular lips, these glasses are extremely prone to breakage. Six martinis at one table might wipe the bar out of glassware for a precious 15-minute stretch. Ring in six martinis and just watch the bartender seethe on the other side of the stick. As the server, you're meant to command control over the table, direct a guest to something else. *Sure, martinis are great, but have you ever considered a VODKA SODA?* Not all guests can be manipulated into the sale of the moment, though, and anyway, I was a young server with little ability to twist one order into another one. I didn't yet know that martini could be converted into *specialty cocktail* by the power of persuasion.

Head dipped low, I went to retrieve my martinis. Six martinis can't fit onto a small cocktail tray, due to their size. Larger cocktail trays are harder to manage. You can't hold them with one hand flush to the bottom, which is how most trays are held: arm at a nearly 90-degree angle, palm flush to the tray, weight balanced onto the center of the hand. My larger tray was unwieldy. It was covered, too, with a white serviette, a cloth napkin meant to conceal the rubber bottom of the tray from guests.

I wobbled through the dining room, glasses clinking, but upright. But just as I arrived to the table, tragedy struck. One martini shook and then fell, knocking the others over like dominoes. Two, three, four, five, all six martinis fell over on the tray, soaking me in alcohol. Dripping wet, I stood in front of my guests with my mouth slightly agape, not unlike a hooked seat bass.

"Martinis! Martinis!" the guests had been chanting,

right up until the moment that the tray had upended onto my chest. They looked as surprised as I did to see six empty glasses and an ever-widening puddle of ex-martini surrounding my feet.

"That's OK!" one woman said. "Tell the bartender to just make 'em again!"

On my days off, I went to the bar, occasionally, to sit and talk to Bill, and also to order food that I had never thought much about until I started working at Bar Americain. A few handfuls of hot, homemade potato chips, served with a hot, homemade blue cheese dipping sauce—this relatively banal dish felt important to me. Before I set foot in this restaurant for the first time, I hated blue cheese. I hated the smell, the consistency, the very sight of it. When it was first placed in front of me, this dish, I wanted to slide it back toward the other side of the bar, but I couldn't; it was a gift. In the hospitality industry, when free food arrives, you eat it. You eat it even when you hate it. You eat it as a sign of respect. I tried it. It was molten. It was complex. I liked it. It made me think about what other foods I had been scared to eat. (There were millions, it turned out.)

Nineteen years later, if you were to ask my friend Bill about those chips, he might not remember that he served them to me. He definitely wouldn't remember that I didn't eat blue cheese when I was 25 years old, that it was one of a long list of foods that I found scary and offensive. Bar

Americain helped open the door to a world of culinary possibility. I stood at the raw bar with Bobby Flay and learned how to clean and eat a whelk. I spilled my first tray of martinis. (Probably not my last.) I learned what was in a Kentucky hot brown. And, more importantly, I learned that it was essential to know the details of the food that I was serving. That ice cream! That vanilla! Burgundy? It was a region. Of course, I knew that. In six weeks, a crash course in fine dining gave me the tools—and, OK, fine, the guts—I needed to work in New York. I fell for fine dining, in a fast, furious, and unexpected way. I fell for it because the world of fine dining made me feel like I was important, even if I wasn't. I fell for fine dining because it was beautiful and glossy. I was learning on the job and loving almost every minute of it.

It's easy to become addicted to restaurants when you're having the time of your life. This is how addiction begins, after all: Things are fun, and exciting, and dramatic, and you don't see the warning signs until you're already very deep inside of a world that's hard to leave. I loved my first years in restaurants, and for good reason: They showed me a side of life that had never before been accessible to me. The food! The wine! The celebrity guests! It was all so incredibly exciting, and, even in the retelling, I feel lucky to have been a part of it.

That feeling—of being lucky—was an essential part of my emotional development in restaurants. It wasn't just luck that I felt, but also a heat, a rush, a warmth on the floor. It was like being set on fire. I was changing as a person in restaurants, or I had already recently changed, from my old days at the Grog to my days at Bar Americain. I wasn't that plain Jane waitress who poured Cavit Pinot Grigio from a magnum, or served Long Island iced teas to thrifty guests on a Saturday night bar shift. This was big-time service, *fine dining*, and I was living in the apex of it, working for a celebrity chef, heading out for one drink, two drinks, four after work.

I was, too, part of the cool crowd who headed to Park Bar on 15th after work, the crowd who knew all of the important people. It wasn't just Boo anymore—I was invited to join in the party, too. Park Bar was dark, with mirrors above the bar. You could barely see the bartenders. You could barely see the door to the bathroom, but everyone seemed to know where it was, and who they were talking to and what they needed when they were in there. It was a throbbing kind of place, small and concise and pushing people together. New York, in 2005, was to the point. After hours, we wanted to get drunk, and quickly, an effective exclamation point at the end of a long night at work. Nothing had to be cute or distinctive. We did not need *cocktails*. We needed *drinks*, cold and fast and hard in a dark room where no one would remember much in a few hours anyway. Bars like that reminded you of the vessel of your body, put to work on the floor of a restaurant night after night, the hard work of it, the hassle, the joy, the delicious first gulp of a cold and utterly tasteless Bud Light.

Maybe I didn't notice the bag of coke slipped from one

palm to another after hours. Or maybe I did. Maybe I was in those bathrooms, too. We weren't there to do anything harmful, we didn't think. We were just having some fun, taking the edge of the edge off. Maybe it didn't seem so bad if the sun was coming up by the time I got into a cab to head back home over the Queensboro to my apartment. The slide from exciting to dangerous was subtle. But everyone slips eventually, and the slow change from restaurant excitement to restaurant danger is what gets people in trouble—it's what got me in trouble.

I worked at Bar Americain for six weeks until, one night, a manager named Colleen caught me texting from my flip phone outside of the bathroom and fired me on the spot. I begged. She was the kind of restaurant lifer who hated people like me—newbies, people who fit in seamlessly for no good reason.

"A rule is a rule," she said, with cruel little eyes. Her hair was blond and straight and oily and she had worked at a nondescript Chelsea restaurant before Bar Americain called the Rocking Horse Cafe, which served average Mexican food. She wanted to be friends with the hot male servers, but they all said mean things about her behind her back and were nice to her in person, mostly so she would give them the best shifts, and I mostly felt sorry for her, for the way she wielded her limited power, thinking she was doing something important, thinking she was solving some problem.

"I won't do it again," I told her.

"Too late," she said, turning on her heel. She wore open-toed shoes, I noticed, a violation of another rule, this one a standard-issue restaurant rule meant to protect anyone entering a kitchen from unsafe conditions. A rule was a rule unless it applied to her. I understood the message. The lesson was a useful one. Don't trust in the power of second chances. Do trust in the power of hypocrisy.

It was summer when Colleen let me go, right around my birthday, late August. I fled into the thick, hot night with my Kate Spade messenger bag slung over my shoulder. I didn't have a plan. I didn't have any savings. Whatever I had made at Bar Americain had already been spent on a combination of rent and partying.

Don't worry, a few of my Bar Americain friends told me. *There are tons of jobs out there.* They happened to be right. The city—majestic, even emptied out as it is in August—was full of restaurants. Demanding, brutish restaurants. Or, from my still-optimistic perspective: untapped reservoirs, culinary destinations, so many damned restaurants! Bar Americain didn't want me, but there were so many other places that would, places where I could practice carrying a tray of martinis, places where I would know, now, to ask the chef about whether or not the ice cream was homemade, places where I would be able to perform better. I had more knowledge, more interest, more passion. A match had been struck. The restaurant world would watch me burn.

*   *   *

White Burgundy–Braised Chicken

Serves 4 to 8

8 bone-in, skin-on chicken thighs
Kosher salt
Freshly ground black pepper
2 tablespoons all-purpose flour
1 tablespoon olive oil
4 medium shallots, thinly sliced
4 garlic cloves, crushed
4 stems fresh thyme
1 cup (249 grams) white Burgundy (inexpensive, like a wine
    from the Mâconnais)
1 cup (240 grams) chicken stock or broth
1 tablespoon cold unsalted butter, cut into cubes
½ cup chopped fresh flat-leaf parsley
2 tablespoons fresh lemon juice
Thin slices of lemon, for serving

Preheat the oven to 425°F.

Season the chicken all over with salt and pepper. Place the flour in a bowl or bag, add the seasoned chicken pieces, and seal as needed. Turn or shake to coat the chicken evenly, then shake off any excess as you pull out the coated pieces. Discard any leftover flour.

Heat the oil in a Dutch oven or other large, heavy pot over medium-high heat until it shimmers. Working in batches, add the chicken, skin sides down, and cook for about 5 minutes on each side, or just until golden brown. Transfer to a plate.

Add the shallots and garlic to the pot and cook for 2 or 3 minutes, stirring often, until they begin to soften. Add the thyme and white wine and bring to a boil, stirring with a wooden spoon to dislodge any browned bits. Reduce the heat to medium-low and cook for about 4 minutes, until the liquid has reduced by two-thirds.

Return the chicken thighs to the pot, skin sides up, along with any accumulated juices. Add the stock or broth, which should not completely cover the meat. Once the liquid has heated through, cover tightly and transfer the pot to the oven. Braise for 20 to 25 minutes, until the chicken is almost cooked through and tender (registers 155 to 160°F on an instant-read thermometer, inserted away from the bone). Uncover; continue to roast for another 8 to 10 minutes, until the exposed chicken begins to crisp up. Use tongs to transfer the chicken to a (clean) plate to rest while you make the sauce.

Return the pot to the stovetop and bring the liquid to a boil over medium-high heat. Cook for about 3 minutes, stirring once or twice, until it has reduced to about 1 cup. Discard the thyme stems and remove the pot from the heat.

Add the butter, half of the parsley, and all the lemon juice to the pot; whisk or stir until the butter has melted and forms an emulsified sauce. Taste, and season with salt and pepper, as needed.

Transfer the chicken thighs to a platter. Spoon the sauce (and garlic) evenly over them. Scatter the remaining chopped parsley and the lemon slices over the chicken. Serve hot.

3 | CELLAR RAT

Thierry Sighel, who had once worked as a clown in the Belgian circus, took my résumé and folded it into a paper airplane. "If this lands over there, past the table, you get the job," he said in a thick accent. "If not, you don't." The airplane soared, way past the lacquered tables, and far beyond the heavy-bottomed chairs on the mezzanine, where we sat. I was hired. It was just that easy.

The job was to work as a captain at Laurent Tourondel's newly opened BLT Prime on East 22nd Street, in Gramercy, a slick restaurant outfitted in competing shades of beige and brown. Downstairs, beneath a skylight, one modish aesthetic feature defined the time, a three-foot-high "blackboard" menu made from black felt, where the restaurant's largely static choices announced themselves in sometimes-shifting white lettering. BLT had taken a note from of-the-moment spots like Cookshop, way over on the West Side, a hot brunch spot where people like James Gandolfini loved to hang out. Farm-to-table was in, and everyone wanted to know where you had *sourced your produce,* and whether or not *ramps or fava beans* had come to the *market* yet (no, not in October, my friends). There was a pulsing obsession with knowing one's farmer. Tim Stark, owner of Eckerton Hill Farm in Pennsylvania, became such a sensation with his heirloom tomatoes at the Union Square Greenmarket that he sold a book chronicling his journey. Even if your restaurant was a steak house, it was your duty to the public to dig into the ethos of the moment: farm-fresh produce, daily jaunts down to Union Square to ponder the meaning of life through a rainbow of vegetables, a willful dedication to the earth and all of its crops.

BLT, of course, was mostly just posturing. Before the restaurant—a carbon copy of its Midtown sibling BLT Steak—moved in, the space had housed the momentarily famous restaurant known as Union Pacific, where one-time celebrity chef Rocco DiSpirito got his start. In 2003, two years before I set foot in BLT for the first time, NBC aired a reality television show called *The Restaurant,* following the then-37-year-old chef through the trials and tribulations of opening an Italian restaurant. The show lasted a year, and Union Pacific closed shortly thereafter, but the space was ground zero for a new generation of chefs on TV—a migration from the genteel, instructive personalities who had cooked on the Food Network without conflict to the young and brash class of fame-seeking chefs with robust, star-making potential that rose in the 2000s. It started at Union Pacific. I was right there, in the middle of it, and I didn't even know it.

But I picked Union Pacific-slash-BLT out of a hat, upon the recommendation from a friend who knew only that there was an opening and that I needed a job, and badly. I was on the heels of a major failure and I was already wary. I wasn't exactly a veteran, but I had worked, by now, at two hometown restaurants and one big-city one, and there was, implanted in me already, a tiny seed of mistrust. You could get punched in the face at a restaurant. You could get fired without a backup plan. You could go into work one day feeling like you had the security of another paycheck, of tips, of money to pay the rent, and you could leave a few hours later with your belongings stuffed into a handbag standing on West 52nd Street wondering how long it would take to find something else. You could even show up to work and arrive to find a thick rope of chain woven through the door handles. What was it to work in a restaurant? Surfing a wave? Existing on a perpetual seesaw? Up and down, we never knew what the next day might hold, and this unpredictability was fascinating and thrilling and intoxicating. Anything was possible. It was also endlessly scary. I was always scared of waking up in the morning without a next day, and that's because it had already happened and, I must have intuited, would someday happen again.

During my years in restaurants, managers—mostly men—told me I needed to develop a thicker skin, and, in some ways, they were probably right. There is no place for the humanity of emotion in restaurants, but I'm not going to pretend that's a normal reaction to circumstances. The fact that people are stripped of their ability to feel after years of working in restaurants is only a response to pain. You can live through trauma—through losing a job over and over again, or through being told you aren't good enough, or through just being gaslighted in the smallest and most imperceptible ways—and turn into stone. You can become inhuman, sub-human, a different human entirely.

In my early days at BLT, though, I was still sanguine. I had hope. Every day when I showed up at work with my chocolate brown men's button-down shirt, my black trousers, my striped silk tie, and my butcher's apron, cinched at the waist, I believed in the electricity of restaurants, and that's because, for all its faults and inauthenticity, BLT was electric. The Grog had been electric, too, even when it hadn't been, and I carried with me the feeling that all restaurants thrum at their best: a precise euphoria indescribable to people who don't love restaurants and unmistakable to those who do. Before BLT, which stood not for the sandwich but for Bistro Laurent Tourondel, the namesake chef had been given three stars at a formal Upper East Side spot called Cello. His bistro marked a tack toward casual cuisine, steaks served in cast iron, tiny cookies served at the end of the meal, Yorkshire puddings that the chef insisted on calling popovers in lieu of bread service. The music was loud and the lights were dim. When my uncle, who had lost hearing in one ear, came to dine, he made a pained expression. It could be a difficult restaurant to enjoy if you didn't like excess: excess noise, excess food, excess drink.

But many people did like those things. Celebrities liked us, and we liked to cater to them. We liked the glossiness of it, the enchantment of fame. Was that Michael Strahan, player for the New York Giants, practically falling into the dining room at a two-top, his quads so protrusive you had to snap yourself in two just to pour the water? String-bean Jimmy Fallon, who lived just around the corner, claimed to be allergic to mushrooms, and possibly that was true or possibly he was just one of those people who lied to save face so that he could avoid copping to the fact that he was one of those people who didn't like a food that most people did like. Gwyneth Paltrow, Chris Martin, Jay-Z, and Beyoncé, seated at the best banquette on a Tuesday night, ordered a bottle of 1996 Latour, a $600 wine to go with the $300 Wagyu steak. Gwyneth paid with an American Express black card, a heavy titanium square that bore her name, and then she tipped ten percent, the icy little troll that she was. But I liked the story anyway, this miserly star who couldn't even bring herself to do the decent and just thing.

Even though I now knew a little about Burgundy, thanks to the education I had never asked to receive at Bar Americain, my wine knowledge was still abysmal. "Columbia," my moniker at the Grog, had of course gotten me nowhere good, but it had been proof, I believed, of some brand of intellect. But wine, with its matrix of regions, grapes, soil types, and language barriers, left me feeling like one of the backups from Thierry's circus days. During a pre-shift meeting one day, the chef, Marc Forgione, the mohawk-topped son of culinary legend Larry Forgione who would go on to star in *Iron Chef America*, wheeled out a filet mignon Rossini, seared steak topped with foie gras, truffles, and a rich Madeira-based sauce.

I looked at it. The dish made sense. Steak: seared. Likely finished in a pan in the oven. The foie was a lobe, not a torchon, also seared, with a caramelized crust on its exterior. The mound of meat sat stacked several inches tall in a ruby-red sauce, reduced, I guessed, on the stove, before it had been spooned over the meat. The truffles, black, had been shaved before us on an adjustable metal mandoline, I could describe the Rossini, I realized, in great detail, if need be. If a guest needed to know the texture of a filet, say, as compared to a rib eye, I could explain the softness of the meat, how lean it was, how it came from a less worked muscle of the cow, the tenderloin. I could talk about foie with delicacy, how it melted into the steak like a cap of butter, how the truffles brought the best parts of the earth into the dish.

"Sell the dish to a table. Anyone," Forgione said. He looked around the room. He settled on me. "You. What your name. Go ahead. Sell it."

I stood up. I described the dish in painstaking detail, pretending that Marc was a table. I could see him falling in love. I was winning him over. But just then, just when I was right about to close the sale, a question came from behind, a thick accent, almost French.

"Now what wine would you pair with it, *Anna*?"

Wine? What wine? I had no idea.

I stumbled over my words. I tripped. I tried to remember the name of the Cabernet in the bottle on the bar downstairs that I had seen walking in. It had a tree on the front. Was it a redwood? People liked to drink Cabernet with steak, right?

"Redwood Cabernet," I said.

"Ah have no idee what zis is," Thierry said. Later, I would learn about his collection, about his love for old California wines, about his well-developed palate, and about how he knew the different vineyards of Burgundy. It had been Sequoia, not Redwood. Sequoia Grove, in fact. I remembered now. I sat down, my face hot.

Whatever shame I betrayed, Fred Dexheimer, BLT's beverage director, who would become a Master Sommelier during my tenure, must have seen it. He looked a little like a 1970s porn star, with overgrown, shaggy, dirty blond hair and a mustache that dipped down a beat too far; he could probably wax it into a handlebar if he wanted to. Fred fancied suits that would have been considered out-of-fashion to an earnest fashionista, but the way he wore them kind of made sense. They were beige, or dark brown, and his shirts had color and pattern and pizzaz. He was just a few years older than I was, but had the sense and sensibility of someone who had been in the business a long time. He had paid his dues.

Lingering on the mezzanine for a minute after the service meeting, Fred asked me to come over. He looked at me and offered what would turn out to be one of the great opportunities of my life. "Come here a second," he said. "Wait, hold on."

He disappeared for a moment, down the mezzanine stairs and back down into the bowels of the restaurant. A few minutes later, Fred was back, this time with Colin Campbell, the restaurant's sommelier. Colin and I had only just met a few days before, but something about him felt familiar to me, like I had known him from another space and time in my life. He wore black glasses and a tight-fitting suit, a thick-knotted tie, and a pastel-colored shirt. His teeth were slightly purple. He had been tasting through wines with a rep.

"I have an idea," Fred said. "This involves you, too, Colin."

"What is it?" I asked.

"You don't know shit about wine," he said. It wasn't a question. He was just stating facts. I wasn't used to being the person in the room without the answers. In fact, I was used to being the opposite, the arrogant know-it-all who always came equipped with a categorically correct set of facts, perfect for establishing myself as the truth teller, the source of information. I had been put in my place by people who clearly knew more than I did, and it was humbling, and horrible. Fred saw this in me; it is the job, after all, of a sommelier to make an immediate assessment of a guest, to sum up the opposition in just a few rough sketches. He had parsed me correctly, had sniffed out my weaknesses and had figured out how to convert them into assets.

"I don't," I confessed. I didn't have to say the quiet part, which was that my lack of knowledge was embarrassing.

"Maybe we can change that," Fred said. "You come in once a week on your day off—what is it, Tuesdays?—and you work with Colin in the cellar. You're a cellar rat."

"A what?"

"A cellar rat. That's what we call it."

He wasn't trying to insult me. Cellar rat is the colloquial term used in the industry to describe the people who spend time stocking the wine cellar. It was where my wine education officially began.

I purchased a copy of *The Wine Bible* and commiserated with Colin and Fred, who had grown up of humble origins in Pennsylvania. Fred wasn't much of a foodie; he ate things like cheese sandwiches on white bread. But if you wanted him to talk about wine, he could tell you the difference between the soil in one vineyard of Burgundy's Côte d'Or and another. He could close his eyes and know the vintage. And if you gave him Chablis and Pinot Grigio side by side in a blind tasting, he was sure to start swearing.

Fred was my unofficial mentor, a person who knew, I suppose, that I was smart enough to do more than upsell glasses of Cabernet to wealthy bridge-and-tunnel Saturday night guests who wanted their filets mignons cooked butterflied and well-done. Eventually, Fred handed me and my wine education off entirely to Colin, who began by making me read all the labels in French.

"Promise you will not make fun of me," I pleaded.

"I won't," he said.

I read *Chassagne-Montrachet* from a bottle, pronouncing every consonant.

Colin laughed so hard he started to cry.

On one of those days, as we dug bottles from boxes and moved inventory to make space for new wines, we tried to place one another. It felt like we were old friends, but it began to occur to me that perhaps it was more than just a weird feeling of nostalgia.

"I swear we know each other from somewhere," I said.

"But you were never in Colorado in college," he said. Colin had gone to Colorado State in Fort Collins and was two years my senior. I hadn't gone there.

"No," I said. "And we're not the same age anyway."

"True," he said.

"Maybe we would have met somewhere else," I said.

He had spent a summer in the city, he said, but no, that wasn't it; the dates didn't match up. But then he mentioned a friend, and something about it felt familiar. His friend, he said, had been studying abroad in London in 2000, and he had gone to visit for spring break.

"We saw Paul Oakenfold spin at this club called Home," he said.

"You're kidding," I said.

"What is it?"

"I was there," I said. "That's where we know each other from. I think I have a picture of us all together."

Our friends—my friend from college and his from Colorado—had dated through high school, and a big group of us had ended up in London together, wild and rowdy and just getting a handle on our miraculous and unshaped lives. That Colin and I had landed back here, in New York, at the same restaurant and in the same cellar seemed like some small and weird miracle, two people flung together.

"It is strange," he said, before tearing into me again. "But, you know, I have to tell you, I'm going to need you to say *Chassagne* one more time."

My wine education was like this: funny, fun, and, in some ways, a reminder of what I have always been best at, which is academic proficiency. If Colin sent me home with an assignment (*read about Graves!*), I came back to work the next day ready to astound. I went to the store and pored over the racks and racks of Bordeaux, imagining the vineyards and their underbellies, the gravel, the taste of wine running through stone. I bought the bottles I could afford and sat in my Astoria apartment and dreamed of what it must be like to live a life that permitted access to all these good things: the finest wines, the deepest cellars, the hedonism of this intellectual pursuit.

The cellar, of course, was our testing ground. I wanted to know what gravel tasted like, what it meant to have stones rolling around in the mouth. Could you taste the minerals? Did it feel like licking a driveway? Colin let me pick the medium-priced bottles for staff tastings. In the hazy half hour before the dining room opened, we sat together and opened bottles and learned. I could taste the rocks of Bordeaux, the gas station fumes of older Rieslings, the ripe raspberries of Vosne-Romanée (if there was a cheap enough bottle). I learned about the dry tannins of Tannat—a grape that grows in southern France and Uruguay—from drinking a bottle of Madiran. The tannins swept across my teeth, puckering my lips. Cabernet Sauvignon from California was "juicy"; that's what we called the Sequoia Grove, which I had finally committed to memory, and it's how I learned how to describe it to guests. Sancerre, from land with streaks of limestone soil, was "racy" and "bright." Every day was an expanding world of taste and vocabulary, an expanding world of learning to drink and savor and know wine.

Every day, I woke up with an excitement buzzing inside

me. How lucky I was to have this job! How lucky I was to be able to do this for a living! My work was exciting, the restaurant, come service time, was its own small addiction. The lights would grow dim, the music would start, and we would begin the business of the second phase of our day, the choreography of the evening, the pace, the rhythm, all of it timing, all of it fast but measured but magnetic but drawing us together but you couldn't stop. That was the thing about working in restaurants: you just could not stop.

BLT, too, was its own force field. It had been the backdrop for a reality television show, and sometimes it felt like we *were* on a reality television show. Sometime during my first year at the restaurant, a toothy drama unfolded. It was great television for anyone watching (was anyone watching but us?). Back then, some guests still paid with large sums of cash. One of the servers had somehow gotten ahold of a manager number, making it possible to void entire checks. When there was a cash payment, the server would go into the computer and void the check with the manager number, then pocket the guest's cash. (A void, it should be noted, in restaurant parlance indicates an item that has never existed at all, while a comp is an item that exists but that the restaurant has absorbed the cost of for one reason or another—perhaps an item was dissatisfying to the customer, or a restaurant wants to show deference to a celebrity or regular by sending out a free dessert. In this case, it would be "comped," to reflect inventory changes.)

Anytime an item is voided, the computer—this program was an Aloha point-of-sale system—tracks not only the void but which manager is inputting the void. At the end of the night, when the checks are tallied, each manager has a certain number of voids and comps attributed to him, her, or them. Only managers are able to do these things, and servers have to call managers over to get permission to make any changes to checks. Some of us knew that one particular server was robbing the restaurant blind, night after night, walking out with fistfuls of cash. After a while, it became a collective operation. A few of the servers worked together, sniffing out cash checks, managing to void them without getting caught (by now, they'd strategically memorized more than one manager number), and pocketing the money before anyone was the wiser. Of course, like most heists, this one was due to unravel, thanks to the Aloha system.

I showed up to work one night only to see the cops dragging several servers away in handcuffs. In the back, where the front-of-the-house and back-of-the-house changed from street clothes into our uniforms and stored our bags and clothing in middle school–esque lockers, I begged for the gossip.

"What. Is. Going. On?" I needed to know.

"We think Jimmy Haber called the cops on their asses," one of the servers told me. Haber, it had long been reported, was basically the restaurant version of a mobster. He was Jewish and kept kosher and he loved to show up at the restaurant with a wad of bills so thick it actually hurt to watch him extract it from his pocket at the end of a meal. The CEO of BLT Restaurant Group, Haber was also the head of Juno Investments, a private-equity firm. In 2004, Juno Investments had acquired AO Precision Manufacturing, a leading supplier of M-16 and AR-15 rifle parts to the US government. If it were me, I wouldn't steal from Jimmy Haber, a man who probably didn't care all that much about the lives of a few pipsqueaks at his Gramercy steak house.

Even with the specters of Jimmy Haber and the restaurant's other owners hanging over me, I loved my job. Other people I knew had to suffer through the pain and rigidity of traditional office hours, and here I was, doing the most fun things with the most fun people, learning about the peccadilloes of celebrities in between learning about the peccadilloes of grapes. The passion for wine kept me going, a red-hot fire burning in me that fueled one day, the next, the day after. It kept me believing, fully, that I was on the right track.

But after service, I was still a *restaurant person,* staying out until the sun came up at a karaoke place on 19th, or instead eating dinner at four in the morning at French Roast, which stayed open all night. You could make a lot of really bad decisions in New York after a night of service, and there was no one to stop you, because everyone was right there making the same bad decisions with you. Who was I to say no to a few after-service shots? Who was I to say no to the occasional bump? We worked so hard, after all. We were just blowing off steam.

It wasn't really my fault when my brand-new chartreuse coat from the Barneys Warehouse sale and my purse that held my car keys, house keys, and wallet got stolen from the back of a barstool at three in the morning when I had walked away and left them to go to the bathroom. I blamed that on the person who would steal someone's coat in the dead of winter and not, of course, on the fact that I had been stupid and drunk enough to abandon every single important thing I owned as I stumbled into that dark and sticky room to pee. And of course it wasn't my fault that I was late for Thanksgiving at my dad's house in Westchester; I had worked late the night before and then somehow ended up at an apartment on 14th Street, but these things happen sometimes: you go out, you drink a Bud Light, two, three, five, ten, and then collapse in the yellowing dawn in an unfamiliar bed only to sneak out in the early gasp of morning, not knowing—you will only know this so many years later—that there are only a few Thanksgivings left, but no one can tell the future. I certainly couldn't.

My job and my life were starting to fuse, but I was 25 years old, and everyone I knew was doing exactly what I was doing. Years later, hot girls and guys would actually profit from it when a reality TV star launched a show called *Vanderpump Rules,* based on the very lifestyle that I was living: The idea was to toss a camera into the mix of a busy restaurant, where tempers, alcohol, and the overshot nerves of glamorous servers in Los Angeles all combined to make for arresting television. It told a gritty truth about restaurants that, when peeled back, showed the lives of the people who worked in them: they were just like ours. We took our work home with us because of the strange and unrelatable hours we kept.

Everything slowly began to revolve around work. The time that I spent at work exceeded the time I spent anywhere else. My free time was spent with people from work, and the lines between work and fun became blurred. Soon, it was difficult to see how I could do anything *but* work in this industry. My normal friends—the ones I had gone to college with, for instance—had jobs that occupied the spaces of regular life. On their days off, weekends, they did grown-up things, like go grocery shopping and pick up their clothes from the dry cleaners. I never saw them anymore, because they slept while I worked, and they ate while I danced through the dining room.

In restaurants, there is a language, a rhythm, a way that you move your body. When you leave the dance of work, even for a day, you still move your whole person as if you're still there. My father would be cooking dinner, perhaps, on a rare Sunday night that I happened to have off. Perhaps the restaurant had too few reservations on the book. Perhaps I had been cut. Squeezing behind him and the kitchen island, the language of the restaurant slipped through into my other life, my home life, my family life. *Behind.* That's what we said in the flurry of service, because if you didn't constantly announce your presence, the corporeality of yourself, there was a chance that a tray, a glass, a meal, could go flying into a guest or a chair or another server. But in my father's kitchen, with so few obstacles and an album—maybe it was Little Feat, or Bonnie Raitt, or Springsteen, my father's favorite— scratching from a record player in the background—there was no true need for this ingrained language. And yet. I carried it with me still, this imprint of my other identity, of who I was becoming in the city, or of who I had already become.

In some ways, my deepest regret is that, while I was going into work and tying my tie and making sure my hair was pulled back and arranging my pens and my wine key and putting my clogs on and straightening out the wrinkles in my black slacks, I loved it so much. Within six years, my father would be gone. Fewer than 2,000 days, if you added them all up, and, really, picking apart every single one of those days and nights, that did not seem like very many at all. How many of those 2,000 nights did I perk up to loud music, running around to entertain strangers? How many nights was I one of the last trickling customers at a dive bar, willing the party to continue just a little bit longer? My dad was still working. He was a lawyer. He had a life to lead.

On occasion, he met me in the city for Chinese food, or came to my apartment when I called him with alarm. *I saw a roach!* He would drive in, the father of daughters after all, and hunt for the perpetrator, which most likely had been dead anyhow, dispose of it, take me to dinner, then drive back to Westchester, a white knight. Since my apartment was small with no real storage, he came to Queens twice a year to rotate my wardrobe, delivering my winter sweaters or my summer dresses. Back to the suburbs in vacuum-sealed packages half of my closet would go until the next seasonal shift.

Every Passover, refusing to force upon me the indignity of the New Jersey Transit, my father detoured through Astoria with my stepmother and two younger sisters in tow to pick me up en route to my grandmother's palatial, gaudy seder in Central New Jersey. It was ceremonious to hear him swear his tight, little swears as we faced holiday traffic each spring, all the way from the BQE through Staten Island.

"Never again," he said. "Never a-fucking-gain." But the swearing, from him, always felt forced, because he was mostly a person who appreciated swearing but didn't do it much himself, unlike my mother and me, who took to bad language, who embraced the utter expression of it, who rolled the words around in our mouths and spit them through our teeth. Anyway, he didn't mean any of it. He would have picked me up at the end of the earth if I had asked, even if I was living a life on a distant planet, which was basically the truth. My life was Martian, alien, abstract to anyone who woke up in the morning and shaved clean and slapped on astringent aftershave and looked right in the mirror and returned to a job that had not changed in nearly 30 years.

"Do you think I should open a bookstore?" I asked him

once. It was before I worked in restaurants, another fit of restlessness, of not understanding where I belonged.

"I think it's a great way to lose a lot of money," he said.

"Probably," I said.

"If you really wanted to do it, I would figure out a way to make it work."

He was determined, I think, to figure out a way to help me make it work at my new chosen profession, too, far away from books and writing, far into the dark night, behind the velvet ropes at dance clubs. I ended up at Marquee one night after work, on Tenth Avenue, at a table with bottle service, and when the girl I was with couldn't find her coat, she looked around in a booth near ours, plucked one out of a pile, and simply pulled it on. The coat was long, with a fur collar, and it was nice enough.

"You're just going to take it?" I asked. It was almost exactly what had happened to me with the chartreuse coat that I had gotten from Barneys Warehouse. I had only owned that coat a couple of days before it disappeared.

"It really isn't a big deal," the girl said. She was a nurse, the girlfriend of a server that I knew. Her name was Christine, or Christina, and she had terrible false eyelashes made from mink and even worse fake boobs. I hated her, but also I wanted her to like me, for no particular reason, or probably because she was thin and popular with the people I worked with and because she went to places like Marquee, places that I ordinarily wouldn't have given a shit about but that people around me seemed to give a shit about. She didn't strike me as particularly smart, but there was a razor's edge to her, a necessary cruelty that did not match with her professional choice. *Nurses are caretakers,* my mother had said to me once, when I had briefly dated one in the early 2000s. But Chris wasn't interested in taking care of anyone, or that wasn't what it looked like in the strobing glow of the club. I asked the same question a second time, about the coat, but I was slurring my words, and I wasn't going to die on this hill. It wasn't my coat. I was making a weak plea, nothing impassioned.

"They'll just take somebody else's," she said. It was ruthless, and I didn't try to stop her, not necessarily because I thought that she was right, but because there was something elastic about the ethical space that we existed in. I didn't fight very hard because it was just a lot easier not to, which was the way it was, not just at Marquee, but everywhere: It was easier not to push back when someone sliding up behind you at the Aloha system grabbed your ass. Was it sexual assault? Would anyone believe you if you said that it was? It was easier to look the other way if a bunch of waiters stole cash checks, even if the tip attached was yours, too. God forbid you were the rat. Better to just wait it out and see what happened in the end than to violate your coworkers like that. It was better to be silent, that was what we had all learned, better to swallow the secrets whole and dive into the darkness, because in the darkness you were anonymous. You were no one. Christine,

Christina, Chrissy, was going to take this thing, and somebody else was going to take this thing, and it would all even out in the end, and that logic seemed to make sense to me at four in the morning on the deep West Side of Manhattan, through the milky gaze of a bottle of Grey Goose.

With my clock turned upside down, I started to see a world where anything was possible—or nothing was. When you have Tuesdays off, and the streets are quiet, and the only people you see are the ones who are also industry, you begin to think that the whole world is divided between people who work in restaurants and people who don't, and developing an exit strategy isn't so much an imperative as it is a distant reality. And so you party on, raging into the night, sleeping well into the day, rinsing, and repeating.

Even if I was embracing a little too much of the unsavory side of the social scene, I was still rising in the ranks. I was a captain at BLT, not a *server*, a distinction that commanded respect. Also, my wine education was beginning to pay off. Colin had stopped laughing at my pronunciation of French wine. We were making progress.

We spent mornings in the cellar, and, on the first of the month, I made it a point to come in to spend the entire day assisting with inventory, counting every single bottle in the entire restaurant and keeping a tally on a form affixed to a clipboard. My side work, the drudgery every server knows—folding napkins, polishing glassware—became exclusively wine-related. It was now my job to slip updated pieces of paper into the leather-bound wine lists; to collect all the Riedel decanters and to make sure they were clean and accounted for; to restock the wine pull according to the inventory list; and to help educate the staff on the wine-by-the-glass list in advance of service each afternoon. I had brought my long-standing academic role as teacher's pet into the restaurant with me. I took the prized seat next to management at the start of each meeting. If I came a little late, it was naturally forgiven; I was likely in the wine room, making sure everything was stocked for a busy night. My priorities as captain were now subverted, and I was sure to let everyone know how important I had become.

During service, if Colin was too busy to make it to a table with a list open, and if I had the time, I went over instead, gently guiding guests to wines I was familiar with. Other servers who found themselves in the weeds—an expression all servers use to describe the inescapable feeling of being in over one's head when it's busy—flagged me down to sell wine to their tables. I used basic wine vocabulary and price points to determine what I should sell, and I took cues from Colin.

"I need you to move this Verduno Pelaverga from Fratelli Alessandria," he would say, and I would do it, talking up the wine based on what I knew: that it was made from a bright purple, thin-skinned grape from northern Italy; that it tasted like bright raspberries and that it was delicate and playful; that it took well to a quick chill; that it was one of the best bargains on the list at well under $50. Pretty soon, I was flicking Colin away when he dared approach my tables for assistance with wine. I wanted to do it myself. I wanted the rush of selling something expensive and challenging, a prize that would make my fellow captains drool, something I could taste at gueridon, something that had been sitting around for decades, something with history. Selling a bottle was an opportunity to taste a bottle, and I saw every open wine list as just one more sign of untapped potential, just another chance to get to open and taste something I had never tried before. The massive wine list betrayed so many secrets. I wanted to know them all.

It was a different kind of rush, selling wine. It activated a part of my brain that had fallen dormant, the part of my brain that had been aching to sit up and scream with life again. In college, ping-ponging between classes and centuries and entire schools of thought, I had always been amazed at the threads of connection between what I was learning. How could it be that Western civilization, so long and so full of material, could stretch its fingers into every crevice of my forming brain? I could be in a darkened room, nodding off to the Gregorian chants, and then it would hit me, in another room, days later, about how those tonal and almost weeping sounds had made their way into the texts of Chaucer, the iambic pentameter, a separate kind of sound, this rhythm on the page and not in the echo of church.

I had tried to get back, again and again, to the place

where my brain was on fire, where it felt like I could under-stand the world and its strings, all pulled together at once. Restaurants hadn't quite been enough for me, until wine, the intellectual pursuit that kept me out of an office and also kept my brain busy, kept me feeling like I was learning some-thing, pushing toward something. On the floor, I was fueled, better and better and better at sizing up a guest, more fluid about the regions of France and Italy and Spain. I studied maps and appellations, came to understand the lexicon and its peculiarities. In the Franken region of Germany, a green, rounded bottle called the Bocksbeutel is used to hold Ries-ling. Translated to English, the word means "goat's balls," and the bulbous bottle, if you think about it long enough, does have a kind of scrotal shape.

"I like a buttery wine," a guest would say, and I would dig into the squiggly, gray part of my brain and dig out words like "oak," and "toast," and "char," words with description and words that could tell a story in just a few seconds, words that were likely to sell a bottle that no one had ever heard of to a person more likely to order Kistler's Les Noisetiers than anything else. A person like that wanted something round and full, a white wine that could touch every single part of the palate and that tasted a little bit like freshly baked bread or a juicy poached pear. They might like a full-bodied Viognier from the northern Rhône valley, in France, which always smelled to me of apricots and orange blossom. Con-drieu. Saint-Joseph. Hermitage Blanc.

I was surprising myself every day with a growing knowledge, maps imprinted in my memory, color-coded regions like the slides that popped up in the dim theater in Art Humanities at the end of my freshman year of college, when we had been asked to memorize the friezes in the Greco-Roman tablatures. And like the details of Rembrandt's self-portraits, and like each pink and coral and orange rhombus in Picasso's *Les Demoiselles d'Avignon,* the magnificent piece that heralded the start of modern painting. Those pieces of art had entered my mind and never left, and so, too, had the vineyards of Châteauneuf-du-Pape, with their rocky landscapes framed by the area's Roman castle, high on a hill.

At first, I was good, and then I was great. I had sense memory. I had unlocked a tiny mystery in wine, the way I had long ago unlocked a mystery in food. At one point, I supposed that I had not known what rosemary smelled like, but now it was as familiar to me as the smell of my own kitchen. Pinot Noir from California was supple, crushed strawberries that had been out in the sun. A Bordeaux from the right bank of the Garonne almost had a plummy quality—end of summer plums—when you got past all the clay from the soil. It went on like this, if you smelled and tasted wine like this, one after the other, the blackberries and sharp black peppercorns in a glass of Shiraz from Australia, but then the same grape, called Syrah in France, and now it was just a hint of bacon when it hits the frying pan, and asphalt, too, the way it smelled when your flip-flops sank into it on an August afternoon.

"You could be great," Colin said. We started thinking about a future—my future—and, all of a sudden, I wasn't destined, necessarily, for a life in the one-dimensional tracks of service. I had a purpose, and it was to study, to take my level exams through the Court of Master Sommeliers, and to become what he had become just a few years earlier: a person in restaurants who was something more than a restaurant person. Was it an excuse I was telling myself, that the pursuit of a position of gravity in a place where so much swirling around me was unserious, would make me a more serious person? The truth was that I needed something to ground me. I often came home and looked through job listings and tossed and turned at the idea of taking a low-paying job in editorial that would lead me, somehow, into a field that related to what I wanted to do, which was write. The idea of trading in the glamorous life that I was living at 25 for a rigid, 40-hour workweek for menial pay was more than I could conceptualize.

The framework of a serious job within the convivial backdrop of a restaurant seemed like something I could wrap my mind around, though. I could do this, I thought. I could advance here. I could make a nice life for myself. I could be the best at this. Colin seemed to think so, too. Where there were opportunities, he pushed. He encouraged my interest. Management noticed my command of the language of wine. Even Thierry—poor Thierry, who had barely hired me but for the whim and whimsy of a paper airplane, and who had watched me stumble so fully through a staff meeting when asked what to pair with a simple Rossini—began to applaud my hard work.

"You're not bad, Anna," he said. I took it as the greatest compliment. I took it to mean that I might have a shot at success in restaurants after all.

*   *   *

Filet Mignon Rossini
Serves 2

This preparation calls for a truffle slicer—typically a small stainless-steel tool that can be purchased at most restaurant supply stores (or online through retailers like Williams-Sonoma). If you do not have a truffle slicer, you can use a mandoline slicer, set to slice on a fine setting.

2 (5-ounce) filet mignons, patted dry
Kosher salt
Freshly ground black pepper
½ cup (18 grams) dried porcini mushrooms
2 cups boiling water, or as needed
¼ cup (60 grams) veal stock or beef stock (or 1 tablespoon
    veal demi-glace)
1 teaspoon finely chopped preserved black truffle
1 tablespoon unsalted butter

1 tablespoon vegetable oil

2 (1½-inch-thick) slices French bread, trimmed to fit
   beneath the filets

2 tablespoons truffle butter

1 (4-ounce) piece fresh foie gras, trimmed and cut
   horizontally in half to fit atop the filets

¼ cup (59 grams) Madeira

About 10 grams fresh black truffle, for garnish

Season the meat on both sides with salt and pepper.

Place the dried mushrooms in a medium bowl and add just enough of the boiling water to cover. Let rehydrate for 20 minutes. Combine the stock and preserved black truffle in a small bowl.

Combine the unsalted butter and oil in a heavy skillet over medium heat. Once they have melted and heated through, add the bread slices and toss quickly to coat; toast just until lightly browned on both sides, then transfer to a plate.

Add 1 tablespoon of the truffle butter to the pan and cook until foamy. Increase the heat to high, add the seasoned filets, and cook for about 4 minutes per side for rare (120 to 125°F), or 5 minutes per side for medium-rare (125 to 135°F), using tongs to turn them as needed. (Depending on how thick they are, you may want to sear them on the sides, too.) Transfer to a plate and cover loosely to keep warm.

In the same skillet over high heat, add the foie gras pieces, cut sides down, and sear for no more than 90 seconds per side, until medium-rare. Place a portion of the seared foie gras atop each filet; they may melt slightly. Re-cover to keep warm.

Working quickly, discard the fat from the skillet. Return the pan to high heat, add the Madeira, and use a wooden spoon to stir and dislodge any browned bits. Add the rehydrated mushrooms and their soaking water, as well as the stock mixture. Bring just to a boil, then remove from heat. Add the remaining 1 tablespoon truffle butter, stirring until melted and incorporated. Taste, and season the sauce with salt and/or pepper as needed.

Place a toasted bread slice at the center of each serving plate. Set a foie gras–topped filet on top of each toasted bread slice. Spoon the sauce over and around the plate. Use the truffle slicer or a mandoline to shave fresh black truffle over each portion and serve.

4 | THEFT

No place is ever only one thing. For me, BLT Prime, where I spent two years of my life, was complicated. I worked 10-hour days and saw more of the inside of the wine cellar than I did of my friends or family. Bottles of wine, in that regard, became my closest confidantes. My colleagues at work were often the first people I spoke to at the beginning of the day and the last people I spoke to at the end of the night. I loved the way the lights went down at 6 o'clock, the feeling the floor had when the restaurant started to fill up, when the music got a little louder, when the crowd started to buzz.

A place like this can stay with you, can burrow into you, even if you don't expect it to. BLT, a place that was meant to be an ordinary, glossy, mid-2000s steak house, wormed its way into my burgeoning consciousness because it was delicious. I was just discovering food, and the restaurant came along at the exact right time, a thrilling reminder of everything I didn't know about when it came to dining. Even now, nearly two decades later, I think back on the tuna tartare from BLT Prime and it stops me in my tracks. That dish is gone. There's not exactly a way to re-create it. It was made in a stacked square mold: a thin layer of avocado topped with a ruby-red helping of bluefin tuna. The topping, a sheet of crispy fried shallots, was the best part. The tartare sat in a salty-sweet sauce of honey, mirin, wasabi, lime juice, soy sauce, and mustard oil. It was an outrageous dish, the kind of dish that haunts you from the culinary afterlife, long after the restaurant has died.

I agreed to take over the beverage program when Fred was promoted. After passing the Master Sommelier exam, Fred advanced to service director for the company, which included BLT Fish, a few blocks to the west, and BLT Steak, on 57th Street. The restaurant group was also expanding its footprint in places like Puerto Rico and other Caribbean outposts. We were gaining national presence, and Fred was at the helm. Colin, once BLT Prime's sommelier, was promoted to beverage director of the BLT Restaurant Group, pinballing between the restaurants in the city. But Prime needed someone on the floor every night to open bottles, stock shelves, and keep inventory in order.

I had been at the restaurant for over a year and a half when they tapped me to take over as sommelier. It was March. I was offered a salary of $50,000, as well as tips from the floor, business cards, and a company BlackBerry. I loved punching emails out with my thick thumbs from its arcane keyboard, then considered a step up from T9 texting on my flip phone. *Sent from my BlackBerry.* I felt like an actual adult for the first time, with my business suit and wine key, my BlackBerry, and my Very Important Job Title: Sommelier. My first paycheck came to just over $700, and I felt such overwhelming joy: a real salary! The business cards, with their dark brown and gold lettering, came about four weeks later. I kept extras in my suit pockets, thrilled to distribute them to anyone who expressed even an iota of interest. I ordered a leather holder, an envelope to keep the cards in, just another small upgrade from my old life, more proof that I had ascended.

In the first week of May, I got a call, in the middle of the chaos of service, that something had gone terribly and irrevocably wrong. In college, my friends and I had formed a tight knot. We were erudite fools, geeks who liked to drink $4 vodka tonics at a place called the Heights, where our poorly constructed fake IDs, procured from a passport photo shop in Times Square, bought us ersatz entree into adulthood. On Thursday nights, we would tumble out onto Broadway, ebullient in tube tops and black flared pants and heeled boots, smoking cigarettes by the fistful. We showed up in cloudy plumes, dropped our cashmere cardigans over the backs of stools, and stood up on the bar so that we could dance to "Hot in Herre" and "Get Ur Freak On" and "It Wasn't Me."

When the sun blushed over Morningside Park, we ordered breakfast sandwiches from Hamilton Deli. We were invincible. We were free.

I was the youngest in our group of friends, which meant that they had gone out into the world already, leaving me behind in a dorm in East Campus, high on 116th Street, when, one robin's egg morning, I watched the cigarette ember of a tower ash down from the picture window at the end of my dormitory hallway, ironically the tallest point on the island looking down toward what had once been the tallest building, now just smoldering cinders and bodies in its place. My class with film auteur theory expert Andrew Sarris had been canceled, and there was nothing left to do in the city besides wait for reports of carnage. And, so, our youth had already been disturbed. We had lost that freedom—the swaying atop a motionless bar, the late-night smoke, the pink mist of sunrise after a long night partying. It was gone now. My friends had dispersed throughout the city, throughout the country. Some were working for magazines, for newspapers, for banks. One had gone to Washington to work for Senator Schumer. He had been an early success, a political whiz, destined for great things.

My friends from college and I would still see each other, on occasion, mostly in New York. But something portended a sense of urgency when I felt my BlackBerry vibrate against my thigh on that Friday night in 2007. I was in the employee bathroom when the call came through. The bathroom was a sanctuary, a place to cry, to hide, and, more often, to eat stolen food. Like everyone else at BLT, I would purloin food returned to the kitchen on a communal Staub serving platter. Sides were presented in cast-iron dishes in the center of the table for guests to pick at. When cleared, the Staubs returned to the kitchen, courtesy of our largely Bengali bus staff. There, the feeding frenzy began.

"Stop eating garbage!" the chefs barked at us from behind the line, but they couldn't do anything about it. The family meal at BLT was abysmal. For years on end, all of us had eaten nothing but the offcuts of beef. Each day, at 4 p.m., we were greeted by the gristly bits of beef that had been cut off from prime steaks that were later served to men in business suits. These nearly inedible morsels were tossed with whatever other extras happened to be lying around: spare Brussels sprouts leaves; boxes upon boxes of pasta; a stir-fry of carrots and other miscellaneous (and undeniably inexpensive) root vegetables, served over bland and overcooked rice. Our family meals, meant to power us through six hours of athleticism on the floor, were a repository for the kitchen's unusable orts, the garbage that wasn't quite fit for the garbage bin. It shouldn't have come as a surprise, then, that we craved the plump mushroom caps (there were always at least a duo left in the sextet), or a handful of skinny and salty French fries, or a blue cheese–stuffed tater tot. We were unapologetic garbage-eaters, so very hungry, all of us.

I was often in the bathroom, just like everyone else,

shoveling garbage into my face. That's probably what I was doing when I saw that I had gotten a call from one of my college friends. My friend Artie—he had been the one who had gone to Washington to work for Schumer, though he had recently come back to New York after accepting a job as Andrew Cuomo's press secretary—had taken his own life. He was 28.

I sank down with my back against the door. It was locked, and I could hear the chits to the service bar, right outside, gnawing through. Personal pain could not stop the flow of service, the merciless chug of a Friday night. The weekends were busy in Gramercy with the worst kinds of customers, the *filet mignon, butterflied, well-done* customers, the B&T crowd, as we labeled them: bridge and tunnel, carried in from outside of New York, people who came to BLT as some kind of performative act. They didn't care about the food, but they wanted to slam their credit cards down on the table as a signifier of wealth. They tipped poorly. We worked twice as hard for the same amount of money on Fridays and Saturdays as we did on Tuesdays and Wednesdays, and the people were worse. They wanted more of us. They wanted all of us. They wanted puppetry. They wanted pageantry. But there was always another table that needed us, always the feeling that time was slipping away. On another Friday night, a man had asked me if I was single, and my mouth had opened and then shut again, making a silent letter O. I knew there was no correct answer. He must've taken the silent O of my lips to mean something that it didn't. He slipped his wedding band off and set it down at the end of the table.

"Well, tonight I am, too," he said.

It was one of those kinds of nights, the same blustery men in suits, slipping through second and third martinis, grazing their fingers past my ass as I tried to make myself thin or, really, invisible, as I tried to deliver the kind of service that is never seen, never noticed, never commented upon. But I held in my hand, instead, the news of an ending. We had spun out from Columbia in fantastic spiderwebs. We were only supposed to make our futures brighter. They weren't supposed to disappear so quickly.

All of this would have to wait. I would have to swallow it down, Artie's death, the finality of it, the thick pall of his lost potential. He had been dire and tragically funny, but still blooming with life, I felt. Only three years earlier, when his father had died, I had sent Artie a card and had received back in the mail a note on heavy stock with a cobalt Jewish star at the top. Artie's barely legible handwriting was the last tangible proof I had in my possession of his life, his grace to me under his own sad circumstances. Now, his family smaller by half, I thought about that note, about the memorials of life and death, of Artie's lack of faith in himself, and about where all of that had led us.

I worked at BLT for two years, but I mostly remember the ending, the way I went out, the extinguishing of Artie's life and my own traumatic failures. In the months before I found myself in the employee bathroom, when I first assumed control of the majority of the restaurant's beverage program, I discovered that I had an inventory issue at BLT, one that I believed was easy enough to solve with simple math: keep close tabs on product, purchase product for an inexpensive price and mark it up at a standard rate, and make a profit.

Unbeknownst to me, however, I had a considerable issue on my hands with Nick, the general manager, who had been stealing alcohol. When I went to reconcile the reports at night, I discovered that the tequila pars were off, a problem that I, the person responsible for BLT Prime's beverage program, would now have to deal with.

My method of dealing with this situation was a salve that any ordinary person could have told you would only lead to more trouble. But I had been under the spell of restaurants for long enough to lose sight of reality, which is why, the night before my friend Artie's life ended, I was busy killing my career, pouring low-grade liquor into high-grade bottles on the speed rack in an attempt to stanch the bleeding of Nick's stealing problem — a thing I knew existed but that I could not prove. There had been a budget meeting, about a week before, and the numbers had been abysmal. My wine and liquor program simply could not catch up, despite our full restaurant, despite our sales. We had a leak that we could not stanch and there seemed like no reasonable way to explain or fix it.

I had pulled up all of the reports, reams and reams of paper that accounted for each bottle of liquor and how much of it we had in house. On the wine side, there were no inaccuracies. On the first day of each month, when we conducted inventory, scanning bottle bar codes with the restaurant-equivalent of a supermarket price-checker, the number of bottles we had in the cellar matched up to the ones we had purchased and sold. On the liquor side, though, it was a completely different story. Bottles were measured based on percentages. We might buy, say, three bottles of Grey Goose one month and then, at the end of the month, have a half a bottle left. That would mean that the sales records should reflect the sales—either through mixed drinks, comps, or losses (spilled drinks, returned drinks, or other miscellaneous mistakes, for instance)—of two and a half bottles. For the majority of the bottles, the sales reports comported with the existing inventory. But when it came to the Patrón Silver, a specific brand and type of tequila, the numbers were way off. We were constantly out of the Patrón, meaning I was constantly restocking it. Looking back through the reports, though, I couldn't find evidence that we were selling the liquor, which happened to be the drink of choice of the general manager.

"What is happening with the liquor cost?" Keith Treyball asked during an afternoon in late April. He was one of the restaurant group's owners, an often quiet and reserved man who always wore a blazer and a starched shirt. I wasn't afraid of him, exactly, but I knew to be on my best behavior when he was around. Keith didn't appreciate the antics of restaurant work. He wanted to see the flow and symmetry of service, and he wanted to see the numbers, of course, but he had no patience for the clogs or the clashing of personalities. He definitely had no patience for anything that threatened the financial stability of this powerhouse on East 22nd.

"I don't know," I said. "It doesn't really make sense. Our wine numbers are good. They're accurate. We're having trouble controlling cost on one specific item, the Patrón Silver."

"I've looked over these reports, and I'm inclined to agree with Hannah," Colin said.

"Do we have any idea where the tequila is going?" Keith said. He held stacks of paper. He looked down across the bridge of his nose at items and numbers, at columns that simply did not match up.

"We suspect there's an employee-related loss that we can't account for," I said.

Nick looked over at me. He narrowed his eyes. Unwittingly, I had made myself a prime target, just by trying to tell the truth.

"Just fix it," Keith said. "I just want you to fix it."

If, in a restaurant, your profit-and-loss numbers are bad, there are many ways to redeem yourself. You don't necessarily have to get more people in the door. In the case of BLT Prime, where we could easily do three turns a night, turning a higher profit was not a matter of getting more people in seats. When it comes to managing a wine program, specifically, one way to manage profit is to negotiate what's called a case break with a wine distributor. While one case of wine might cost, say, $216, a distributor might be willing to order a "break" on multiple cases: $192 a case for three cases, $168 each for five cases, and $144 each for ten cases. So, if a bottle of wine, purchased at $216 a case, costs $18, it only costs $12 on ten cases. If you have the storage space and a robust wine-by-the-glass program, where you're able to move enough wine over the course of a month, it's worth it to pay up front and take in the inventory, because the savings are obvious. And a wine director would not necessarily be obligated to sell the wine at $12 per glass—wine-by-the-glass is typically sold at the bottle cost price—even though that would reflect the discount. The wine's value, $18, would likely be the glass price, driving up the profit margin for the wine director. With a 5-ounce wine pour, each bottle poured by the glass would yield five servings. Eight glasses of that wine, sold at $18 per glass, would pay for a case of wine on a ten-case break at $144 a case, an astounding deal. The rest? Pure profit.

Liquor, of course, was more complicated. You could buy liquor from the city's two main distributors—back then, Empire and Southern—in split cases, purchasing a bottle, or two, three bottles at a time, reflecting the individual needs of a restaurant. Each pour of liquor, which is typically 1 to 1½ ounces, costs the restaurant 20 to 25 percent, far more than a glass of wine. Depending on the cost of the spirit itself, that spirit would be marked up about 20 percent, but it is impossible to mark it up any further than that because customers simply wouldn't buy it.

A shot of alcohol sold at a restaurant is not, therefore, very valuable to a wine and beverage director. But a mixed drink can be *very* valuable. A specialty cocktail list, with its splashes of cheap juices and twists of fruit, reduces the actual alcohol used. It's a money-saver. All of those drinks with complex names and ingredients are designed to make money, to carry the burden of other, less profitable items.

There is, too, the well.

In the well, the casual drinker will find the least desirable, low-shelf alcohol in the house, the tolerable vodka, the gin that is drinkable if not entirely sippable, the Jose Cuervo. But, no, never the Patrón. Tossed into the speed rack—a metal bin at the bartender's knee level, where a bottle can be easily grabbed, tipped over, and spilled into a glass with near-impunity—these well spirits are bought by the case, because they sell quickly. If a guest orders a vodka soda without specifying the type of vodka she wants, she's getting well vodka, and, on a busy night, that's just fine with everyone.

I had not thought much about the well. Ours had been standard. Absolut for the vodka pour, some entry-level gin, Cuervo, generic triple sec. Each night after service, I printed out the sales reports. There was a Patrón Silver here or there, but no real quantity of it. Still, the bottles were disappearing from inventory, evaporating, as if they'd never been there to begin with.

One afternoon, before the start of service, Colin walked in cradling a box. He held it so gingerly, I was worried he was carrying something alive, something human.

"Look what I did," he said, but I already knew. I had told him not to do it when he asked. It was a Baccarat crystal bottle of Louis XIII Cognac, round and full of caramel-colored liquor. Made from 1,200 different types of eau de vie, the brandy, with its stoppered top, is aged within 100-year-old tierçons, thin French casks that were originally designed for maritime transport and that are no longer manufactured. This baby was not a baby, though we needed to treat it like one. Every single glass of Cognac poured from this baby needed to be poured out into a jigger, measured and then placed carefully into a glass—no spills!—for the world to see. Three hundred dollars. That's what a glass would cost you. Who knew how long it would take to recoup the investment.

"It just seems like a bad idea," I said. I thought about the Patrón, and how we couldn't get a handle on it. I thought about the servers I knew, who were prone to sneaking a shot of something at the service bar during dinner. I didn't begrudge them their indulgences, but I surely wouldn't want them stealing $300 shots of Cognac, either.

"It's fine," Colin said. "Every night after service, the closing manager will take it from the bar to the wine pull, and it will get locked in there until the next night." We couldn't afford to leave it out, couldn't afford the sheer liability of a bottle like that, just sitting out in the open, an easy target.

I don't think we had the bottle a week when I got the bad news.

"I have something to tell you," the closing manager said when I came in the next day. He had a peculiar grin on his face. I thought I was being set up for a spectacular joke.

"What is it?"

"I dropped the Louis," he said.

"That's very funny."

"I'm not joking. I was walking from the bar and I just slipped and it fell. On the slate. Right outside the wine pull." He gestured with his hands. I looked down at the floor, near the wine pull, where I happened to be standing. In the streaming, midday light, I could see a streak on the floor, as if the scene of a murder had been haphazardly cleaned up in my absence.

"Really. You have to be joking," I said. "Because this can't possibly be true."

"It's true," he said. "But I saved you the glass stopper."

The unscathed glass stopper would not be enough to save me from the certain death of the wine and liquor program, I surmised. I now had a $3,000 hole in my program to worry about, in addition to a Patrón Silver abyss. I could take all the case breaks in the world, but I couldn't envision a case break big enough to get me out of the screaming void of the profit-and-loss nightmare that I had found myself in.

"Thanks for letting me know," I said. I was very pale. I resisted the urge to step into the wine pull and vomit all over my treasured Burgundies. Instead, I locked myself in there for a solid two minutes and cried, trying to come up with a solution, wondering where the entrance and exit to the maze were, and how I had gotten the two confused in the first place.

A few days before the Cognac incident, BLT had been contracted for an off-premises catering event. Catering events ran the gamut from expensive to very, very cheap, and this one fell into the latter category. The guests had ordered an unthinkably bad gin, Crystal Palace, a gin so brutally acidic and perfumed with overly potent juniper that even they couldn't drink it. But it was cheap—dirt cheap. Cheap enough to help dig me out of my hole, I thought, if I could find a way to use it.

My idea was unethical. It was illegal. I felt like my brain had been splintered into a million, tiny, ineffective brains. What if I took the Crystal Palace and poured it into the gin we had on the speed rack? What if I cut costs by serving bullshit gin to unsuspecting customers? One of the managers was overtly stealing tequila. This was, to be clear, another version of stealing. I'm not sure why it seemed so easy, opening the black caps, pouring the liquor into a bottle of Bombay

Sapphire, wiping my hands on the back of my jeans, carrying the case down the stairs, pretending that none of it had ever happened. It didn't bother me, probably because I had carried for so long the burden of those stolen Patrón bottles. I was knowingly duping customers from the moment I pulled a Crystal Palace bottle out of the case.

Still, I had been left with the burden of others' mistakes all this time, a 27-year-old with virtually no experience, left to manage thousands upon thousands of dollars of inventory, as the people around me did as they pleased. Reclaiming agency felt personally important, even as it jeopardized my allegiance to honesty. That I knew what I was doing was wrong and did it anyway doesn't get to the heart of what I was feeling at the time: sunk by others' out-of-control behavior; part of a failing enterprise; out of options; scratching for anything that might give me a foothold to survive in my position. Of course, I should have thought harder about how committing a crime to save my job was oppositional, but that just speaks to how jumbled and distressed my thinking was. I couldn't parse right from wrong. All I wanted was to keep my head above water for long enough to make it to the next week.

Hanging above the bar at BLT were cameras, which I thought nothing about. No one really monitored them, except for me and Colin, and he was my ally, anyway. Even if he had caught me topping off bottles, I had faith that he'd admonish the behavior and let it slide. The cameras were there to keep the bartenders honest, but I wasn't a bartender, and this wasn't service. I hadn't thought much about what the cameras did and did not catch, or about their wholesale purpose. My entire criminal act, in fact, was one of desperation and poor conception. Naturally, a few bottles of booze could not have saved me from the deep ditch of loss over profit. Naturally, sacrificing personal ethics for the sake of saving the restaurant a few bucks made no rational sense. Naturally. Had I been in my right mind, I never would have done these things. I wasn't in my right mind; I was in a fugue state, guided by a singular purpose. I needed to save my job, save myself, save the career of diminishing returns. I often felt that I had fallen into the position of sommelier by chance, and I wasn't confident that lightning would strike twice. Where would I end up after this, a former waitress who had briefly been a sommelier, this person who had once had *so much potential,* but who was now blowing it all. Poof.

The cameras caught me in sharp relief, standing behind the bar, unearthing an empty aquamarine bottle of Bombay Sapphire, transferring the contents of the Crystal Palace into it. My features were clear. From above, you could see the part of my hair and the way my back rose up and curved a little toward my neck, the way my butt jutted out. I know how the images appeared from the aerial view, saw them myself after my friend Artie's funeral.

While I was away at the funeral, on the first day I had taken off from the restaurant in months, Nick pulled tapes from behind the bar, hunting, I think, for a way to catch me. A guest, he told me, had sent back a gin and tonic.

"He ordered the Bombay," Nick said, once I was back. We were seated in the basement office, at one of the main computers. He had placed a CD into the disc drive, for me to see.

I nodded. He didn't have to say what came next.

"I tasted that Bombay," he said. "It was really bad. So I started to look at what had happened." The story about the customer could have been true or invented. It didn't much matter now. Before me, on the computer, I could see my own familiar figure, reenacting the motions of the week before: Crystal Palace out of one bottle and into another.

"I see," I said. "What now?"

"Either I tell Keith or you do," Nick said. He was glad, I think, to have caught me in a trap. With me out of his hair, he could go on with his Patrón game, drinking without supervision.

"I'll do it," I said. This seemed to have caught him off guard.

"OK, I'll set up a time for you," Nick said.

"That's not necessary."

Nick looked surprised. He clearly relished having caught me in the middle of something and had tried to control the narrative by reaching out to Jeff Kadish, one of the partners at Main Street Restaurant Partners, the group that owned Calle Ocho, Rain, and Django and that co-owned BLT Prime and the two BLT Steaks in Manhattan and Washington, DC. I wasn't going to give Nick the satisfaction of allowing him to tell Keith, too. I could own up to that myself.

"You'll tell him yourself?" Nick said.

"Yes, right after I meet with Jeff," I told him. I had a good relationship with Jeff, and a little bit of confidence that I could work things out on my own. Nick seethed. I felt good about that.

Jeff emailed me and asked if I could come to his office on West 25th Street for a meeting, and I did. Jeff was understanding and kind. He made no indication one way or another regarding whether my time with BLT was over. He just sort of looked me up and down, possibly assessing the level of my guilt. Then he let me head back out into the late-spring sunshine to sit with my sins.

I sent Keith an email right after, asking if he'd be willing to sit down with me. *Please let me know if you're available; if not, I completely understand.* It was a Thursday, May 24th. Keith told me he was free to speak the following Tuesday morning. We met in the private dining room, where I explained what I had done. He nodded thoughtfully.

"You were trying to save money? For us?" he asked.

"Yes," I said. "I was concerned about the P & L. Especially with the Patrón issue and the Louis bottle."

"You're young. I understand that this was a mistake. You've been with us for a long time. Everyone makes mistakes," he said.

By now, I was crying. "I know," I said.

"Give me a day to discuss this with the other partners, and I'll get back to you," he said. "It's not the end of the world, you know."

I worked a busy service that night. I opened bottles of Bordeaux at gueridon. I poured myself a taste of vintages that had thrived in the sun when I was 6, 9, 10, 16 years old. I poured plumes of wine into decanters and swirled them by candlelight to identify the shreds of sediment that remained, evidence of earth and stone and grape must and whatever else a wine sheds in its old age, the skin cells of wine, its mortality, its shell, the trappings of its bottling. I watched service unfold in slow motion, clipping by in sepia-toned scenes, knowing that this could be my final version of it. Were the chits really spitting from the machine that slowly? In the dim light of the dining room, I could hear the whispers of servers, their incantations: *behind, watch your back, eighty-six, hot plate,* their restaurant patois. When you know that something is ending, you feel attuned to every last muscle of it. I could feel the suede of the banquettes beneath my fingers as never before, the thick lacquer of the tables. Upstairs, in the pastry kitchen, I was assaulted by the smell of the restaurant's petits fours, tiny rounds of chocolate chip cookies made on sheet trays and then cut out in circle molds the size of quarters.

When would I eat another square-molded tuna tartare, another colossal rib eye with its demitasse side of bone marrow, which I liked to spread atop the fire-licked steak. The marrow would nearly melt into the meat, fat on fat, one thick bite after another. It was never enough. The American Wagyu skirt steak, marinated and topped with a garlicky chimichurri—all crunchy greens—was sliced so thin you could practically slip it into your pocket while walking past a table. I never tried this, though I thought about it a million times in the heat of service, when the smell of it nearly brought me to my knees.

At the end of each night, the servers would break down the cheese cart. That cart had been the bane of my existence when I had worked as a captain, but now I regarded it with reverence, too. Selling cheese to patrons—wheeling the massive butcher block through a packed dining room—had not been worth the time or money when I had been in the weeds. But breaking off pieces of Midnight Moon, Cypress Grove's goat's milk aged Gouda-style cheese from California, had saved me on more than one night, had brought me clarity in darkness. Jasper Hill Farm's raw milk Bayley Hazen Blue had taught me to love blue cheese, to love its veins and its funk and its melt, even. I took a final stroll into the kitchen that night, before changing into my street clothes and exiting through the porter's door and out onto the dark, damp street, not knowing what the next day would bring.

When I returned, Keith was not there. The restaurant was quiet. Colin greeted me, wearing a tight suit and a tie knotted into a double Windsor. I could see something tortured in his face. *I feel like a million bucks, run over twice,* one of his friends had said, when we first met as college students at that club named Home in London, where Paul Oakenfold was DJing. Now it was Colin's turn to feel like the million bucks, run over. Soon, it would be mine.

He gestured for me to sit down, again in the private dining room, and then took a seat next to me.

"You know I don't want to do this," he said.

We were friends. We went back more than half a decade. He didn't want to say the thing they had sent him here to say, but they had sent him here because he was my friend, or they had sent him here because they were cowards, or they had sent him here because they thought it would be easier. Either way, they had sent him here, and it wasn't an accident that they had chosen to send him.

"You don't have to say it," I said. "I already know."

"I'm so sorry," he said. "But that was so stupid of you! You got caught! You did it on camera!"

He took my hand. Together, we walked to the wine cellar, our cellar, our sanctuary, where no one could bother us. Colin had installed a clothes rod for me in one corner to match his, where I could hang my suits and dresses. There my belongings stood, Banana Republic suits in black and navy and cream, pin-striped and solid, with matching skirts and dresses and pants. I'd have no use for them now.

I stood looking at the suits. There were so many of them. Colin watched me take in the cellar. In two years, I had collected a lot of stuff: shoes, bottles of wine that were part of my semi-permanent collection, clothing, books. Moving out was just another burden.

"Hold on a minute," he said.

He came back with a stack of brown paper bags, the extra-large ones with the BLT label emblazoned on the front, which we used for takeout. We took the suits down from the rod, folding them into thirds and stuffing them into the bags. We piled the books in, the wine, the Dansko dining room clogs in shiny patent leather. Before me, an impossible mountain of bags appeared, the Mount Everest of work ephemera.

"I can help you to the street," Colin said. When a restaurant fires you, they want you out of the building immediately. You cannot stay to collect your thoughts. You cannot stay to say goodbye to colleagues. Your time there—two years of my life—is over. Make your exit with grace.

Out on the street, spring had arrived in full force. Park Avenue South was blooming. I turned to look at the flowers, petals everywhere, dancing from the bony fingers of recently naked neighborhood trees. Gramercy would go on like this without me now. What excuse would I have to come back, after all. It would be summer, and the young guys coming from Wall Street would roll up their sleeves and order the heirloom tomato salad with Stilton and bacon and a New York strip, rare, and a side of creamy mushrooms, and, while the market was flush, a bottle of Screaming Eagle to prove their machismo. The restaurant didn't need me to survive. It could do it all on its own.

Colin hailed a cab heading uptown, on the east side of the street. "Jump in," he said, holding the door open and kissing me on the cheek. I pushed the bags in first and then dove, face-first, into the car, looking toward the black leather seats, toward the paper of the bags, toward the plastic divider, but never toward him on the corner. I can't remember if he was waving goodbye, or if he had taken off his black-rimmed glasses to massage the bridge of his nose. Up we went, turning and heading north on Third Avenue, past the building my father had worked at in the 1980s—where my mother had gone into labor with me—until we hit the Queensboro, and then, all at once, Manhattan and BLT were both behind me.

I was broken. I had reached what I believed to be the lowest part—and I thought, when I left BLT, that I was leaving the industry. I recognized, for a bit, how bad my situation was at that particular place, but not for long (I'd end up at other places that were just as bad, because breaking up with an industry is a series of misfires, I'd find). During this middle part of my journey, I stumbled emotionally, trying to figure out who I was. I wanted to leave, but I could not leave. I believed that I could work nowhere *but* restaurants, that my worth elsewhere had all but expired (over dinner one night a few years after I finally had gotten out, a drunken family member got too loose with the truth, confirming my worst fears: *Your father never wanted you to be a writer; he just wanted you to go to therapy*).

But during this tender middle, the soft, raw part of my life where I was driven crazy with the desire to be anyone but myself, I felt trapped by circumstance. These places, which were meant to be a stopgap between my successful time in academia and a successful career in the "real world," had smothered me, had demolished any chance for a life. It was impossible to get out. I was beginning to learn how truly dangerous and toxic restaurants really were, and although I was a long way from the end of my journey, this knowledge was formative. I was slowly arriving at the unwelcome conclusion that I was headed in the wrong direction. It was, after all, at this point in my time in restaurants that I began to understand that restaurant work might be hurting me, although I remained far from leaving the industry for good. One consequence of growing up in a house where regular discomfort is normalized: you can keep circling the drain interminably, because you're used to coming back over and over again, to seeking love in loveless circumstances, which is, I think, what I kept doing with restaurants. Toxic workplaces can often mislead us, confuse us, and even convince us that up is down and down is up.

Before I was fired from BLT Prime, I believed that I was untouchable. It's not that I had never been fired before, because I had. But I was a rising star in the sommelier world. I had connections, and high-profile wine-world friends. People knew who I was. I wore a suit to work and was paid a salary. I had business cards. My failure felt like a fall to earth. I had created this situation myself, of course, had been wrapped up in a life that was too much for me. But also, I had reached, I now know, a turning point in my life in the industry. I was treated differently among colleagues afterward. People whispered. Job offers appeared and then, suddenly, evaporated. Later, I would learn that Nick had gone to others and had urged them not to hire me, a practice that, though technically illegal, is cruel and common in the restaurant industry; I was part of a blacklist. I felt one way about my work before this happened, and, after, distinctly another way. I had promoted my industry, had encouraged others to take me and my position seriously. Now, I couldn't even take myself seriously.

I remember, with aching clarity, the feeling of that final cab ride away from BLT, a place that had secured my position in the wine world. Had I destroyed myself, or had it destroyed me? I had felt a sense of obligation, to protect the restaurant at all costs, and this obligation had led me straight through whatever moral code had guided me up until I had arrived at restaurant work. When my friend had died, I had been given no more than a moment to grieve. I had a second in the bathroom to collect myself, and then back to the grind of service it was. I wasn't a human being; I was a worker. The next day, when I told Nick that I needed the day off to be with my friends—that I needed to collect myself in the wake of a specific and unreasonable tragedy—he had balked.

"It's a Saturday night," he said. "I don't have anyone to cover you."

For a minute, I stood looking at him, realizing that he was right. There was no compromise in restaurants. My friends from college had dropped what they were doing to come back, to honor Artie for one night before his funeral. They were going to commiserate and trade stories, to remember the time that he went mountain biking in Breck the day before our friend Megan's wedding, slashing up his knees and ending up in the emergency room. I'd have to beg off.

Then I thought about it again. It wasn't reasonable, to choose steaks in Staubs over humanity. Not this time. I rarely stood up for myself in restaurants. Most people would have said that my personality contradicted the doormat way that most servers and staff are so easily treated in places like this, but, just like everyone else, I was swept through by management, by bad bosses and bad schedules. I stopped fighting back because fighting back would lose you your job and because fighting back just earned you a reputation as "problematic." Once you stop fighting back for long enough, you stop remembering how to fight back, and you give in to the softness of someone else's decision-making. Your choices aren't yours anymore.

Still, something broke in me that day. I thought about an essay that Artie had written for the *Columbia Daily Spectator*, where we both had been on staff. Published on my 20th birthday—August 29th, 2000—Artie wrote about his first year at Columbia, when he was kicked out of housing for putting his fist through a window of the freshman dorm, Carman.

"Beyond the material results, though, I remember quite clearly that on one of those long marches down Amsterdam, well past the neon hours, the reasons I snapped that window were far beyond any perceived misdeed done me," he wrote. "The causal chain lurched beyond those few minutes of intensity, the week prior, choices not made the prior semester, or even to a rainy night the year before when I had refused to act and lived with the frustration inherent. More likely the chain of my stagnant self-hatred included all of them, a culmination of nights, days, and moments when I stood frozen, unable to make myself do the difficult thing that needed to be done, whether it had been kissing a girl or calling someone about a job. And so, when I look back on that spring spent walking the wide avenues of the Upper West Side, I know there's a spot somewhere on Amsterdam between 78th and 116th where I began to fathom the necessity of taking the difficult and uncomfortable actions demanded by this life that if left undone might leave you staring 13 stories down on a streetscape, wishing you were part of the glass cascade."

He had been the architect of such art at just 21, with an abstract understanding of pain, and he had ended up in the glass cascade after all. Where would I end up?

*   *   *

Farfalle with Mushroom-Cognac Sauce
Serves 8

Kosher salt
1 pound dried farfalle
  (bow tie pasta)
12 ounces fresh mushrooms, such as cremini or button,
  wiped clean, stemmed, and thinly sliced
1 tablespoon unsalted butter
½ cup chopped yellow onion
⅓ cup finely chopped shallots
1 tablespoon minced garlic
¼ teaspoon freshly ground black pepper
¼ cup (64 grams) Cognac
¾ cup (181 grams) half-and-half
¼ teaspoon freshly grated nutmeg
2 tablespoons chopped fresh thyme

Bring a large pot of water to a boil over medium-high heat. Add a good pinch or two of salt and then the pasta; cook for 2 minutes less than the package directions indicate, until al dente. Reserve 1 cup of the pasta cooking water, then drain the pasta in a colander set in the sink.

Heat a large, nonstick skillet over medium-high heat. Add the mushrooms and cook for a few minutes, without stirring, until they become fragrant and browned. Add the butter. Once it melts, stir in the onion, shallots, garlic, pepper, and

1 teaspoon salt. Cook for about 10 minutes, or until the mushrooms' moisture has evaporated.

Off heat, add the Cognac. Return the pan to the heat for 2 to 3 minutes, until the Cognac has evaporated. Remove from the heat. Add the cooked farfalle, half-and-half, nutmeg, and thyme, tossing to coat evenly. Add the reserved pasta cooking water, ¼ cup at a time, until the farfalle is completely coated with the sauce. If needed, season with up to ½ teaspoon salt. Serve immediately.

5 | FOURPLAY

When I was 7, my mother married the man who had once been her high school sweetheart. In the first halcyon days of their reunion, this man was kind to me; I loved the child-sized stuffed dog that he brought as a gift the first time we ever met. I named him Sam.

But the man who would eventually become my stepfather turned out to be very different once we were all living together in one house, and once my mother had a second batch of children to attend to. By the time I was 8, 9, 10, he had grown red-faced and mean, annoyed by everything from my breathing to my inefficiency. I got in the way. I caused mischief. I was a snotty, bookish girl who missed her own father, who acted out by kicking the occasional substitute teacher or by getting kicked out of summer camp. I was in pain, but it was undiagnosable. I had been taken away from my father, and now I was marooned with a man who didn't love me nearly as much as he loved his own kids. He wouldn't ever grow to love me in the way he was meant to, and I wouldn't ever grow to forgive him for his faults. Instead, we'd be paralyzed like this, frozen in time, two imperfect people in space.

On occasion, my stepfather was angry enough to chase me around the house and threaten me with a backhand, or grab me by the roots of my hair and wrench upward—I remember the wicked, searing pain—teaching me a *lesson* as he dragged me upstairs. This man, this adult man at 6 feet, 4 inches, bringing a rag-doll little girl up to her bedroom, for she had been bad, in whatever capacity bad means when you are a child. And yet, when it was over, I came crawling back, as children do, desperate for his love.

When you grow up like this, a seed of trauma forms inside of you. The ability to bury trauma would follow me to an adult life in New York. The punishment of restaurants felt familiar. I came back, again and again, to places that punched me down, to places that brought me back to the dynamic that unhealthily mimicked the one that I had been brought up in. When you're small, and you're told that you are the reason for others' terrible behavior, you begin to internalize that you are the reason for everyone's terrible behavior. Without knowing it, that was how I saw my restaurant relationships. If my schedule was inflexible and grueling, it was for my own good. If a man wanted me as his side piece and not as his full-time girlfriend, well, at least it was something. At least I could justify to myself that I had been chosen. I couldn't get out of the way of my sense of self because my identity had been formed around the idea that love and abuse were dutifully connected, and that in order to serve one side of it, you have to accept the other.

I think often of these qualities of mine—regression, concession—when I think of Johnny Iuzzini. He was a famous pastry chef who had not yet made it to television. That would come later. But in 2007, he was known mostly as a prodigy, the Catskills-raised son of a plumber who had somehow ended up at one of the city's top restaurants.

It was only a few weeks after I left BLT. I was working at Jean-Georges, the petite and bourgeois restaurant tucked into Trump's building on Columbus Circle, just off Central Park, where the sounds and smells of New York faded into the austere dining room. It was a room of extravagances small and large—one of the more arresting displays took place when Philippe Vongerichten, the restaurant's general manager and brother of its executive chef, came through with a pineapple. There, in the clear, gray light, Philippe would pierce the end of the fruit with two forks and hoist it into the air, carving ravines into its sides before setting it ablaze with kirsch. This was the kind of performative act that looked better than it tasted. It was, after all, just a very expensive pineapple, and that's how I felt about most of the food at the restaurant: it was pretty, if a little uninteresting, but men in business suits preferred to dine here over many other restaurants, where the silver was turned over so that guests could see the imprint of the producer.

At Jean-Georges, I had managed to land a two-week stage as a sommelier. I had hoped the job would restore my reputation. I had hoped, too, that it would lead to a full-time gig at the group's downtown restaurant, Perry St, a cooler, chicer spot that very much felt like a place where I would fit in. In Gramercy at BLT Prime, we had played loud music and dimmed the lights at 6 o'clock. Further uptown, at Jean-Georges, the mood was stodgy. In the dining room: no leaning. Business was conducted at a whisper. If a guest got up to use the restroom, one did not fold a napkin in absentia, as was protocol in nearly every other restaurant in fine dining. Instead, that napkin was removed, a mark of a lack of decorum. *This dirty thing!* A new one appeared, folded beside the plate, as if by magic, before the guest reemerged.

There is a difference between restaurants that receive two or three stars from the *New York Times* and restaurants that receive four. At restaurants that receive four, like Jean-Georges, waiting tables is a career because the money allows it. The job was demanding, but it offered rewards in return. This was not an entry-level restaurant job, and others in the industry understood the level of discipline and professionalism required to work at a such a place.

The line between fine dining and extremely fine dining is one that many don't see. Guests aren't interested in learning about who you are. Your personality isn't the reason they're here. The top-tier dining rooms of Per Se and Jean-Georges and Le Bernardin are rooms where pomp and circumstance reign. If you're used to working in fine dining, like I was, the transition to top-tier can be brutal. There's no pleasure in a four-star dining room, no joviality. You can't be jocular with your fellow servers. There's no room for error. A server is not permitted to do the following: wear colored nail polish; cross hands in front of the body; slouch; speak to colleagues on the floor; carry a glass from the bar to the table without a tray; show visible tattoos; wear hair in an inappropriate manner (this can be at the discretion of a manager); touch a glass by any part except the stem; pour wine in the incorrect order; spill; laugh. Sometimes, I could feel the rising crest of a snicker, a guffaw, a full-on parade of laughter in my throat. Fine dining wears those feelings down to a soft, dull nub. The things that may have felt funny—so funny you can't contain them—become less funny over time. Eventually, you learn to swallow every sweet, sour, and rusty emotion. Eventually, you learn to imitate a statue. Eventually, you learn you're not imitating any longer.

Jean-Georges is a place defined by its traditions, pineapples and all, and so it is a place defined by its regulars. When I worked there, Tim and Nina Zagat, the couple responsible for the highly regarded Zagat restaurant guides, came in to dine multiple times per week, for lunch. Tim, a rotund, grotesque man who savored traditional French dishes like brains à la Grenobloise, procured from his jacket pocket at every possible occasion an extendable fork, which he would use to stab into food that belonged to his guests. It was his dining table, this act was meant to say. *Your food is my food. Don't even try to deny it.*

Though the restaurant was a departure for me, there was something silently charming about Jean-Georges. If you love service—or were, as I was, addicted to the inherent charms of restaurants—you couldn't help but love this one, with its old school customs and precise technique. To enter the dining room was to enter another world, which is, at its core, what fine dining is all about: transportive experience. To be in there, among the most expensive wines in the world, with the carts and tableside plating, the French-style service and the whisper-quiet, was to be in elite company. Do you know how to decant a bottle of 50-year-old wine over a candle so that the sediment remains in the neck? Do you know how to fillet a fish in front of a guest, removing the tiny bones with no more than a fish spoon and fork? Do you know the rules of serving and clearing plates? Such is the pinnacle of service, and honestly, we treasured it.

Reviewers at the time lauded Jean-Georges's creative dishes. The lambs' brains, which were tiny—no larger, on the plate, than the palm of a child—were never my favorite. They were slippery and gray, and before service I had walked by an entire tray of them once, laid out on a sheet tray: just brains, a discomfiting notion. But I did fall instantly in love with the restaurant's foie gras brûlée, a savory puck of duck's liver, rolled au torchon, dusted in a fine layer of sugar, and lit aflame. A brittle layer of cracked caramel yielded to the spoon, and beneath: indulgent, fat foie, one of the luxury items that you could find lurking at every brasserie in the mid-2000s. A disc of brioche, more butter than bread, held the whole dish together. Savory. Sweet. Creamy. Crunchy. Fatty. A stand-in for both appetizer and dessert and endowed with just a hint of acid. (From where? I don't remember.) The dish was a reminder—then and still—that a restaurant can have a long legacy. Pick a dish as a postcard. If I were to return to that dining room, I'd request the brûlée.

Chef Jean-Georges Vongerichten, the critically acclaimed Alsatian chef responsible for the restaurant, was himself a perfectionist. As if the kitchen were not already immaculate, at any point throughout service, there was the mop and bucket, ready to be wielded at the pass, the narrow gap that connects the kitchen with the front-of-the-house. At Chef's behest, the floors were mopped, arresting service, but maintaining the gleaming white. Mark Lapico, then the chef de cuisine, stood in the room in the brightest chef's whites, marred by not one molecule of food, his Prada slip-on shoes a far cry from the Dansko clogs worn by most kitchen employees. Service slipped around at a grumble as opposed to the growl and churn that it did at other restaurants. Lapico checked the incoming orders from the thermal printer with a Sharpie that lived in his biceps pocket.

Had I ever seen another place like this, where food was produced, yes, but where, in truth, there was no grimy proof of it, no accidental leak of ketchup, no grease trap overflowing on occasion, no tipping over of tray or sticky floor that betrayed months—if not years—of old food? There was no cacophony, no clang of pots, no shouting or anger or indication of the stress that comes when the printer is operating in overdrive. You could draw a line from the start of service to the end, and the meal was predictable and even: a blooming flower at places where tables were sat; an even cadence of meals, easily looked after, served, cleaned, rinsed, repeated.

In this sense, Jean-Georges was a sort of parallel universe, a place where food was crafted with precision for an audience of people who believed in an art of extreme performance. It never smelled like actual food at the restaurant. Prep all took place in the basement, and the quick work of plating was nothing more than a two-step. Out the door food went, before it even had a chance to register on the senses. The truth was, you didn't come to Jean-Georges to hear the sizzle of a steak or to smell a meal en route to a table. You came for the creaminess: creamy white tablecloths, creamy gray carpeting, creamy nondescript banquettes, creamy sauces, creamy blank French nouveau cooking, the creamy and fattening and tiny portions of the very wealthy.

It was always a surprise, then, when dessert arrived, plated on a square vessel with four quadrants, the most avant-garde part of the meal. For all its formality, Jean-Georges set its pastry chef, Johnny Iuzzini, loose in the final course. The quadrants were often interpretations. Sometimes these were ingredient-themed, and other times they were seasonally inspired. Consider a rumination on rhubarb: in one quadrant, a birch beer soft-serve ice cream, served in a tiny glass with carbonated strawberry-rhubarb consommé. In another, a rhubarb panna cotta with dried rhubarb powder. Then, a jade-green matcha cake, surrounded by hibiscus and red wine–poached rhubarb. Finally, an orb of crispy rhubarb cheesecake, topped with a dollop of raspberry puree. Each tiny square was its own symphony, its own composition of texture, flavor, and color. You could muse over it, could marry minuscule bites in various ways until you'd expanded the possibility of how many flavors could be combined. Johnny's artistry was expansive, moving well past what anyone expected.

Guests lost their minds over these desserts. *New York* magazine's profile fawned over the chef, who admitted to such an aggressive sugar addiction that, by 2003, he had worn down his teeth completely and was replacing his veneers every year; he was only 29 at the time. It was the age of the hip, young male chef. All around the city, the coolest spots were being defined by brash young personalities, the Marc Forgiones and the Rocco DiSpiritos of the culinary world. The city was moving toward a more youthful dining outlook, in ways that even Jean-Georges had to reckon with. The Dover sole was still deboned, plated, and sauced tableside. But the dessert? It flew off in a million directions, a weird composition of flavor and colors, not unlike Grant Achatz's painted experience at Chicago's Alinea, where the chef covered the table with a rubber cloth and produced a Jackson Pollock–esque edible painting in front of diners' very eyes.

Jean-Georges was a restaurant that favored rigidity, but not when it came to that final course. The pastry department held a certain power. Perhaps the rules that we were confined to upstairs in the dining room (*don't slouch!*) did not apply in patisserie, where celebrity chef Johnny Iuzzini was so dearly beloved that an explosion of colors and flavors—four quadrants, indeed—was allowed to rub up against the tidiness of that fine dining experience.

Johnny Iuzzini began his career at Jean-Georges in 2002 after working under François Payard for several years at Daniel and Café Boulud. A year after beginning at Jean-Georges, Iuzzini won the James Beard Award for Outstanding Pastry Chef. Two years later, he would publish his first book, called *Dessert FourPlay: Sweet Quartets from a Four-Star Pastry Chef.* That was one year after I met him in the basement of the restaurant, where he operated a glossy pastry kitchen, as well as a fully refrigerated chocolate locker, where he created the final tastes of the evening, handcrafted chocolates (he would later go on to open his own single-origin chocolate company).

Unlike the straitlaced servers on the floor, Johnny Iuzzini was a slick character, with a gelled pompadour, a Ducati, a gig spinning as a DJ downtown on occasion, and a chic apartment in the East Village. His slickness could be attractive, a combination of kitchen machismo and a general disregard for fine dining convention, which I appreciated. On the first or second day of my stage, I had been sent downstairs to meet with Johnny by the director of operations to learn more about the restaurant's pastry program, down to the bowels of the seemingly endless restaurant. The prep kitchen, pastry kitchen, chocolate unit, employee dining café, and lockers constituted an underground maze, never-ending passageways to spaces that hide staff from guests. In the chocolate room, I was meant to learn about the procedure of making the tiny petits fours that go out to guests as the final gift each evening. Instead, in the room so cool that my breath took on the condensed look of smoke, I stood statue-still as Johnny grabbed me from behind. Maybe I didn't mind.

Restaurants, it should be said, are sensual, a place where food and bodies are constantly coming together. "Behind," we say, whenever we need to alert another server or staff member of our existence. It's a precaution, an insider alarm; we don't want to catch anyone unawares. But there are indiscretions that are acceptable in restaurants, too: hands on hips to gently cajole a person out of the way, a brush of the shoulder, a caress of the thigh. This is what it means to be in a tight space with other human bodies. You learn to see your own body as no more than an object. A hand on a hip is only a hand on a hip in the service of moving an object out of the way.

Except sometimes that wasn't the case, like in the choc-olate room. Being grabbed from behind was more than a hand on a hip. There was a club, Johnny said in my ear, and he was heading there after work. Did I want to go, too? In the kitchen, the system of order is called a brigade. At the top of the brigade: executive chef, chef de cuisine, sous-chef. From there on down, the brigade accounts for the cooks on the line (the cook who runs the cold station: garde-manger; the cook who breaks down protein and works on entrées: entremetier; the cook who works sauce: saucier). The pastry chef, or patissier, is its own position, with its own section of the kitchen and its own hierarchy. Johnny was the boss of pastry, the head of the department. It was hard not to view this as power. Did the patissier actually have any authority over the front-of-the-house? Technically not. But in the chill of the chocolate room, arms wrapped around my torso, it felt like power. It felt like being chosen by Willy Wonka. It felt like not having a choice at all.

"Come downtown with me," he said.

Chocolate must be kept cool because it is such a shapeshifter. Chocolate-making involves rules. It involves process. You have to temper chocolate. If you fail to control chocolate, it will turn chalky. It will lose its texture and sheen, break prematurely, turn grainy in the mouth. Such a delicate material, chocolate, far more delicate than pastry, or even pastry cream. That Johnny had chosen chocolate, this most temperamental of ingredients, as his passion project, felt meaningful. Why choose the thing that is hardest, I wondered? It must take a patient person—a person with delicate hands and constitution—to choose to work with something so infinitely fickle. Here was an artist, I thought. Here was someone who had chosen such a difficult medium, chocolate of all things. And he wanted me to go downtown with him. He wanted me to accompany him into his secret, private life, away from the restaurant, into the bright and charming city. How could I possibly decline?

"We have to go separately," he said. "No one can see us."

That should have been my first red flag.

All employees at Jean-Georges leave through a separate entrance, so that the guests don't have to mingle with them; this is another rule of fine dining. When service has ended, and you are in your plain clothes, you must disappear into the night, through a porter's entrance or side door, a performer who has played the role. No one can see you in this real life of yours, this city life, where you wear jeans and sweaters and carry a backpack or purse. It would destroy the magic of a restaurant for a guest to know that you are a human being, the kind who eats food and drinks wine on occasion, and who, god forbid, uses a bathroom.

Outside, it was spring or early summer. I remember there were blooms in Central Park, and that I had gone running midday, in a break between shifts, one lower loop in the hour that I had away from the restaurant, four quick miles in the breathless and warm air. I remember it was warm, too, when I left through the loading dock; I hadn't needed a coat. I remember a streetlight reflecting on water, black ink on the city sidewalk. Johnny got on his Ducati, a fast bike that would beat me downtown. I hailed a cab on Central Park West, and headed into the velvet night.

Johnny liked to dress up. His club outfit, which he must have changed into before leaving, reminded me of Elton John: a silver bodysuit, platform shoes, big glasses, his iconic pompadour. We had drinks and listened to music. No one knew me there, but everyone knew him. Everywhere in New York, in 2007, people knew Johnny Iuzzini. This young, rock-star pastry chef was a hot commodity, and this made me, his date for the evening, equally important. To go out into the deepest parts of the city on the arm of a chef was exciting, probably just as exciting as working in restaurants. No doubt the club scene brought Johnny some of the same thrills as the pulse of the line when the tickets move so fast that they just about run into one another. I did not think that I was being manipulated, or that the invitation to come downtown was untoward. I thought only that I was being invited to see a part of New York to which I had never before been granted access. That invitation felt precious, and I felt unworthy.

You can look back, in retrospect, and realize that you were a fool, but those self-determinations are easier to arrive at way after the fact. That night, I felt like Johnny's hard-won prize, even if I had done exactly nothing to earn the title.

When he asked me to go back to his place, the invitation felt like a natural extension of the evening. Outside, the sky was turning from black to violet. He got back onto his Ducati; I took another cab. What time was it? Had dawn crested yet? New York stayed open too late, and we had all the time in the world. There was no box of chocolates back at his East Village apartment, no cake or plated dessert to await me; chefs are known for their bare cupboards, and his cupboards were noticeably bare. Johnny talked about his mother, who had died the year before, at 56. I would think about this later, from time to time, about what it had meant for him to lose her, about whether it made him a sympathetic character in the wake of my own losses.

He had seemed forlorn, sitting on his couch in that apartment as morning started to blister through. She had been so young, a veterinarian's assistant, still living in Upstate New York. Johnny seemed to be baring his soul, and I was young enough to believe that this meant something more than it actually meant, that he was opening up, that he was revealing something tender, some soft side of himself that looked the way that I imagined his chocolates did in the center, the way they showed what they really were when you bit into them. Two years later, when he was 55, my own father would be diagnosed with ALS. I would know the crushing sadness of it, of losing a parent young, of trying to be normal, to be decent, of trying not to be terrible through terrible tragedy, of making myself smaller and smaller until I felt like

I had failed to exist in a world where his illness took every breath.

But Johnny wasn't any of these things. He was not normal, or decent. He did not try to be less terrible through terrible tragedy. He used death as a crutch, I think now, to expose a nerve and then cover it back up with a hard shell. It was a ruse, a way of baiting me and others because he knew we could be baited. What I think about, more than his mother, is the title of his book. *FourPlay*. It haunts me. He thought it was funny, the idea of four desserts on a plate, this intersection of sex and sweets, the idea that he could just get away with it.

Johnny led me into his bedroom.

There were the things that I agreed to and the things that I did not agree to. What I agreed to: sex. What I did not agree to: the camera that appeared out of nowhere. There was no permission to grant. Johnny had already started filming. I looked up from the bed and was greeted by the cold, blank stare of a camera, and not of a partner.

I told him to stop. In my head, I thought about the things that I could do, or the things that I could say, about the obvious betrayal. I thought about how disgusting it was, about how I could end up on the Internet, about how I could never run for president, and about how ridiculous that thought was, since I had never planned to run for president in the first place. My brain ran on hyperdrive, firing at a million thoughts a second, and my mouth ran dry. *Stop* came out, a pathetic, one-syllable word, but what I meant to say was *Get the fuck away from me* and *What the fuck is wrong with you?* but none of those things seemed to be able to come tumbling out when I needed them to. I was a dried-up river, born of the same connective tissue as some rag-doll girl who had asked that same stepfather who had yanked on my chestnut hair to wash it, with attendant tenderness, in the primary bathroom. You can feel two things at once, and I did, pulled in two directions, like a dog toy that has been ripped at the seams until it barely exists anymore. *Stop. Don't stop. Stop this, but stay here, with me, because, please, I do not want to be alone.*

"If you don't want your face in it, you can put a pillowcase over your head," he said. He didn't put the camera down. He was staring at me from above, holding the camera in one hand and holding his hair back with another. He wasn't exactly standing upright; it was more of a kneel. Still, he could have pinned me down if he wanted. I wasn't free to leave, the position said. This image is mine, the position said.

I didn't agree to the pillowcase, either. I didn't want to be a floating sphere, a headless apparition in his dreams. His foreplay—fourplay, it turns out—was a woman without a head, appearing in his bed without a face. A bag over my head.

I don't know why, but I didn't leave. I felt like I couldn't somehow, like I was pinned by an invisible hand. Or part of me wanted to stay, to win his affection, the way I wanted to win my stepfather back after an argument that had never been my fault to begin with. Johnny didn't press the issue of the pillowcase again, but his face twisted up, and the version of him that had been with me until then—the chocolatier who was fun and pleasant and who missed his mom—had vanished. This Johnny was angry. This Johnny had been denied something he wanted, and I got the feeling that he was unaccustomed to denial.

In the blush of dawn, at Johnny Iuzzini's apartment, I was a girl again, or just my same adult self, crafted in youth: this is who you are when abuse takes hold in your youngest years. The shame of that moment was eclipsed by another emotion blooming inside of me. This felt like something I already knew, the feeling of having to concede, the feeling of losing the fight, of withering, of allowing another person to pull and pull and pull until you are just a lifeless piece of dough, hollow. I was hollow.

It didn't feel like any ancient betrayal, being photographed without consent. It felt like the same thing as always, just another person whom I had trusted who had let me down a little. Johnny was another power imbalance to negotiate, another calculated loss.

I often think that I stayed in restaurants because restaurants were the natural place for a person like me, a person who was constantly seeking affection in places where affection was simply unavailable. Ruthlessness may not have been beautiful, but it sure did feel familiar, just like waking up in Johnny Iuzzini's bed. When I think back on all the situations that I never should have been in, I think, too, that I was conditioned to find myself there. It was no accident that I came into restaurants seeking the love that had been denied me in childhood. I was looking for something, peeling myself back like an onion without realizing that an onion eventually falls apart. The center cannot hold without the outer layers.

The morning after my night with Johnny, I went back to my apartment to change. The light reflected off of subway cars on the elevated train on the way to work. Those trains, they looked very, very clean, and I felt very, very dirty, a situational crisis that I realized was not exactly my fault—or was it? I had to wonder if I had put myself in a position of vulnerability, another reminder of being a little kid (*you asked for this / if you hadn't made me so mad*). It's not just trauma that walks with you in the haunting moments after a night like this. The true feeling, if I were to pinpoint it, is shame, and the best way to overcome deep shame is to make yourself believe that it was always your idea: the sex, the drinks, that you had agency, that you were the one who wanted it in the first place. Somehow, that feels less shameful than the truth.

At work the next day, I told a server that we had been out at the club together—nothing about the apartment, the sex, the camera, the pillowcase. Later, Johnny pulled me into the chocolate room, seething.

"You weren't supposed to tell anyone we went out," he said.

"I didn't realize it was a big deal."

"It was. I could get in trouble."

Something about his wrath made me feel even worse. The potential job, the celebrity chef who now hated me, the bag on my head: all of it snaked around me. I took the train downtown on my day off, half expecting to see his Ducati parked outside of his apartment, but it wasn't there. I left a copy of a book on the steps outside of his apartment building door, *Heat* by Bill Buford, wondering if this book—one that connected food and love and travel and all of the things that I thought might mean something—could bridge the gap. Johnny had convinced me of something that I believed to be true, that I had betrayed him in some fundamental way. And I was desperate to win back his trust.

I spent even more time wondering about my own complicity. Was it not my fault that I had been treated like garbage by this celebrity chef, after all? I had gone to his apartment of my own volition. I had made the choice to comingle work and pleasure—against the advice of friends, naturally—myself. Johnny had not coerced me or taken advantage of me in any real way. I could have put the pillowcase over my head. It would have made no difference.

There was a fundamental part of me that felt turned upside down. Was it wrong to be grabbed by a chef during work hours in a chocolate room, even if I liked it? Was it wrong, in the aftermath, for him to have requested my silence and complicity, for him to have issued blame, claiming that if I had said anything that I would be jeopardizing his career? And surely it was wrong for him to have asked me to put a pillowcase over my head, even if it was only some infantile execution of his male fantasy?

But it was all a lie. The truth—I would learn this later—was that Johnny Iuzzini had a long-term girlfriend who worked at a bar on the Lower East Side, and the casualty, in all of this, was me. When he suggested that I put a pillowcase over my head, he really did not want to see my face, the reality of me, the person behind the sex. I was just a girl in a basement who looked good in a uniform. I was just a girl at a bar after a shift. I was just a girl on a couch listening at the right time. I was just a girl whom he could ask to put a bag over her head. I was just a girl.

There were other girls, too. In 2017, four women came forward to say that they had been sexually harassed by Iuzzini at work. It wasn't just me; it was any girl. Every girl. It was my friend, Tia, whom he had propositioned at her Midtown restaurant, even though she was dating his coworker. It was a woman from work who claimed that he stuck his tongue down her throat without permission. It was probably women who didn't come forward, too, or women like me who were not quite sure if there had been a violation or not, but who had spent years thinking that something about their encounters had felt wrong. Was I willing to put a pillowcase over my head? How many others had he asked? How many women had said yes, even though I had defiantly said no?

Johnny wasn't an artist. He was something more twisted, more grotesque. Deep within me, there was a black, hardened tree, branches of which had been growing almost my entire life, the angry scars of mistreatment. There it was: anger. I was so fucking *angry*. Why be afraid to say it, anyway? Probably because a public figure—that's who Johnny was—can make your life a living hell if you dare betray your own humanity. Probably because a woman isn't allowed to be angry if she was a part-willing participant. I should have been thankful for the attention, thankful to be temporarily on the arm of such a hot commodity. He took me downtown, into his weird, little world. That should have been enough for me, but it wasn't. I should have been grateful, but I wasn't. Instead, I was seething, a roiling pot, ripe for overflow.

But yes, I was angry, in the way that women are not permitted to be, angry that I had been fooled, angry that the system of power that had always been held over my head had once more been used to persuade me into doing something that had confused me. I was angry at my own fucked-up feelings and angry that I didn't know how to separate want from need from what was good for me. I was angry, too, that I might have even taken him back. I was angry that I didn't know myself well enough to predict my own emotions. If Johnny had shown up on my doorstep with a bouquet of handmade chocolates—his version of roses, I imagined—Ducati helmet in hand, would I have changed my mind? The truth was, I didn't even know, and that made me even angrier, that a person in power could have so much power over me. Johnny Iuzzini wasn't an artist, I realized. He was a magician holding a balloon and, conveniently, a long needle, getting ready to deflate the fantasy, whenever he felt ready. He had deflated me. I was deflated.

Good chocolate, I think, is both bitter and sweet, at least the way that I prefer it. I don't know whether or not Johnny loved the ingredient for this quality, but it's what I like about it—that it can be two things at once, that it can straddle the palate and remind us of how high a dessert can climb. The artistry that people found so obsessive when it came to Johnny—that he could stew over an ingredient and turn it into four composed desserts—is exactly what I find uninteresting. In the end, those desserts didn't actually taste that good. They were bombastic, and they were visual, and they drew you in. They were tricky and manipulative, the way that restaurants and the people in them can be. But they weren't the kind of desserts that keep you up at night, pierced with longing.

We never needed those four desserts, not any of us.

*　　*　　*

Bittersweet Chocolate Cream Pie
Serves 8

FILLING
½ cup (100 grams) granulated sugar

3 tablespoons cornstarch

2 tablespoons Dutch-process cocoa powder

¾ teaspoon kosher salt

2 cups (200 grams) whole milk

1 cup (227 grams) heavy cream

6 large egg yolks

8 ounces (225 grams) semisweet bar chocolate, chopped

2 tablespoons unsalted butter, cubed

1 teaspoon vanilla extract

CRUST
1 (8.75-ounce) package Archway Soft Dutch Cocoa
     chocolate cookies (or similar)

½ teaspoon kosher salt

4 tablespoons (62.5 grams) unsalted butter, melted

TOPPING
1½ cups (340.5 grams) heavy cream

2 tablespoons confectioners' sugar

1 teaspoon vanilla extract

3 ounces mascarpone cheese

For the filling: Whisk together the sugar, cornstarch, cocoa powder, and salt in a heavy-bottomed pan, just until combined. Add about ¼ cup of the milk and the cream and whisk together until a paste forms. Slowly add the remaining milk, whisking constantly. Whisk in the egg yolks and cook over medium heat until the mixture has thickened and reached a slow boil, about 8 minutes. Remove from heat and immediately fold in the chopped chocolate, butter, and vanilla.

Pour the custard through a fine-meshed sieve, pressing it through with a rubber spatula into a mixing bowl. Place plastic wrap directly on the surface of the custard. Refrigerate until the base of the bowl has cooled, a minimum of 3 hours.

For the crust: Preheat the oven to 350°F. In a food processor, pulse the cookies and salt until fine crumbs form. With the motor running, add the butter in a slow stream until the mixture is completely combined. Transfer the mixture to a 9-inch pie pan and use a ¼-cup measuring cup to pack the crumbs into the pan, beginning at the center of the pan, working outward and pressing evenly up the edges. Bake in the center of the oven for 10 minutes, until fragrant and just set (the bottom will feel soft and forgiving, like a brownie, but will firm up as it cools).

For the topping: In a wide mixing bowl, combine the cream, confectioners' sugar, and vanilla. Using an electric hand mixer on the lowest setting (or a stand mixer), blend the ingredients until the cream is just beginning to thicken, about 2 minutes. Fold in the mascarpone and continue to beat on the highest setting for a minute or two longer, until the mixture reaches a consistency somewhere between whipped cream and cream cheese. Set aside.

To assemble: At least 1 hour before you intend to serve, transfer the chocolate custard to the prebaked pie shell using a rubber spatula and spread evenly to the edges of the pan. Follow this with the mascarpone topping, using either a large spoon, rubber spatula, or offset spatula to spread it directly from the center of the pie and work outward. Refrigerate for 1 hour, or up to 1 day, before serving.

6 | ROCKEFELLER

For a long time, after my time at BLT expired, I was despondent. Jean-Georges was not the right fit, and every other job opportunity that presented itself seemed like a round hole for me, a square peg. I took a job at the Sea Grill in Rockefeller Center during the holiday season of 2007, because there were no other jobs left to take. No one was looking at my résumé anymore. The hippest, most zeitgeisty restaurants didn't want me; BLT had made sure of that. The Patina Restaurant Group didn't offer me the most money to work at the Sea Grill, but they did need a warm body to work through New Year's, and I was a warm body.

At the Sea Grill, you could pay $300 to rent the ice for an hour. Large panels of glass overlooked the skating rink at Rockefeller Center. Guests were always shocked by the sight of the naked ice, the romance, the ersatz love scene playing out before their eyes. First, the Zamboni would glide through, clearing the ice. Next: a beau and his girlfriend; a dozen long-stemmed roses. He would go down on one knee and produce the box, and she would cry and mouth, *Yes, of course,* and the dining room would erupt in applause, and the servers and managers would pretend that this exact scene had not played out every single hour of every service between Thanksgiving and Christmas, and that the roses were not included in the Engagement Package.

Most days, I ran to work across the Queensboro Bridge with a backpack on, showering at the 59th Street New York Sports Club, then working a double before taking a cab home at night. It was relentless, bruising work, rigorous service at its worst: poor tips, visiting tourists in Christmas sweaters ordering Sonoma-Cutrer by the case and pretending not to notice that you're working on a national holiday. There was no time to eat between shifts, so I stole heels of the green olive bread meant for table service and crammed them into my mouth in the employee bathroom, or behind the dish pit, or down in the cavernous basement, where a maze of hallways connected the endless businesses of Rockefeller Center.

I had been there a month—give or take a few days—when Jason slipped a pink paperback copy of Neruda's *Twenty Love Poems and a Song of Despair* into my pocketbook. It was bookmarked with thermal paper, a flimsy heart denoting which poem to read first. The purse was a Marc Jacobs hobo bag, the first substantive purchase I had ever made, thanks to my first major paycheck from BLT. I had walked right into Bloomingdale's and bought the bag, in olive green, which came wrapped in a dust cover. It had cost $495, plus tax, almost an entire paycheck. But I bought it because I believed (I guess I still believe, because I still have the bag) that I had succeeded in some fundamental way: at 25, I could walk into one of the fanciest stores in New York and buy something truly nice for myself. Restaurants had given me that.

And also, even when restaurants were boring and repetitive and stupid (sometimes they were stupid), they were also a club, and I had a key. After work, I could head over to Smith & Wollensky, where only a select few people—the insiders—knew about the after-hours, off-menu international wine selection, with Bordeaux dating back to the 1960s. There, at one in the morning, I could order a bottle of 1968 Mouton Rothschild for under $300 and share it with a friend alongside a bone-in sirloin. I had access to New York society. Without a reservation, I could eat the duck à la presse at Daniel, a dish made from an aged whole duck, with an ancient duck press wheeled out into the dining room to press the duck's carcass for everyone to see in order to make the sauce. At Gramercy Tavern, I could get a late-night cheese plate and two glasses of Madeira, on the house, of course, a symbol of my status. These were conditional perks. Put up with the torment of restaurants and you could get treated like a queen, and sometimes that felt like enough, to go out in the greatest city in the world and feel like true royalty. Sometimes, that was more than enough.

Jason Wagner, who had worked at the Sea Grill for years at that point (was it five? seven?) probably made as much in a single night as my fancy handbag cost, it should be said. His job was unionized, which meant that if he didn't want to work Thanksgiving, so be it. He wore the restaurant's standard dark blue shirt, tucked into belted pants with a tie. His hair was a dark red and he had kind of a goatee that crept up around a well-defined chin. He wore black-rimmed glasses and smelled slightly of stale tobacco, a familiar smell, the kind of smell that feels at home in restaurants. I could see him whisper off at breaks, down through the maze below Rockefeller, where employees filtered in and out. He liked to steal a smoke like everybody else in the industry, and then between shifts he liked to hurry across to Morrell Wine Bar & Cafe, where you could order a few ounces of Barolo—his favorite—for under $20, a gift from the Italian gods.

He had been raised, he told me, in a family of Jehovah's Witnesses, and had defected from the outskirts of Atlanta to Brooklyn. His parents didn't speak to him any longer, and he had given up the tenets of his faith. In youth, he had knocked on the doors of strangers, proselytizing. Perhaps it was this bred-in tradition of converting the strong-willed that made him so good at convincing me to fall for him. His early life, after all, had been colored by the duties of convincing people to do things they had not necessarily wanted to do on their own. I had not wanted to fall in love with him. I told him that from the moment I found the book and the paper tucked into my bag. I didn't need the trouble. I didn't need any excitement, just a job to show up at every day. That was it. But Jason was persistent. He selected poems for me to read, "Body of a Woman" cracking the hard, brittle shell of me, revealing the interior, like a walnut, like something that could be scavenged and eaten and stolen by surprise. He wanted me to know whatever he had excavated before me:

Body of a woman, white hills, white thighs,
You look like a world, lying in surrender.

I hated that it was working. Only a sucker fell for the mediocre efforts of men like this, men who could do the bare minimum and still get to the flattened-out center. Jason, it turned out, found the pin-striped-suit version of me sexy, the way I pranced around the dining room—not the physical detail of it, exactly, but more the position I held. My power. He wanted to be a sommelier, too. He wanted to shed the union position, server at the Sea Grill, and be promoted to wine expert, the one with the Windsor-knotted tie and the smart double-breast who could instruct guests on the hot vintage of 2003 and how it ripened the Côte d'Or in Burgundy, after that terrible European August that killed both overripened grapes and people.

I don't remember when I finally gave in to his persistence, to the Neruda and the love notes and the poetry. One day, I finally just said yes, and then we were in the gray cement cellar, pressed up against a wall in secret, losing ourselves in each other, the smell of cigarettes, of tar and roses—that was his Barolo from a midday sip—of fresh-baked green olive bread from the kitchen upstairs. We could hear the clang of pots and always a door slamming somewhere, always the threat of someone about to catch us, and that was part of what made it exciting, or part of what made it so fucking sad.

At first, I didn't know that he lived with a girlfriend, a speech pathologist, back in Brooklyn. They had a cat and a history and mutual friends. They had a life. At some point, I suspected, and then I must have known outright. They were breaking up, he said. They were on the verge of ending a very long and tired thing. One night, Jason came to my apartment to cook me dinner. I lived in a third-floor walkup, in a one-bedroom that was plagued with roaches, and, for a time, bedbugs, that had no real light save for what bled in through the airshafts. But it was mine, a place where I could hang whatever I liked on the walls, a place where the walls of the bedroom were green because that was the color I had painted them when I had moved in. In the heat of summer, when I ran two air conditioners at once and the aged electrical system gave way, it was my task and my task alone to manipulate a kitchen chair in the dark to find and change those damned glass fuses. The apartment had been a gift to myself, a promise of independence. In renting it, I had proven that I didn't need anyone to share life with. I could manage New York on my own, with my ugly red couch that I had gotten from Jordan's Furniture, and which was way too large for my living room-slash-dining room; with my rolltop desk that had once sat in my childhood bedroom and now sat unused, a marker of my dreams; with my tiny galley kitchen, where I had installed, without help, a series of shelves for pots and pans that I would use to entertain the occasional guest.

To open that apartment up to a boyfriend was to open up a private part of myself. Here were the books I collected, the baseball paraphernalia, the ephemera of my passions. Jason came in on a cool fall afternoon with shopping bags and a bottle of wine and headed straight for the kitchen, pushing past the life I had created for myself, pushing himself in.

"I'm making risotto," he said, pushing me up against the wall first, always pushing. I had believed, at the time, that our relationship was autonomous, but when I think back on it now, I know that something more insidious was at work. I was the brittle-boned prey, just out of my longstanding relationship with BLT, a place that did not love me the way that I loved it. I was ripe for picking, probably wistful and sad. I was stuck on something, on a moment in the past, dragging the baggage of old restaurants with me, and this made me extremely vulnerable to the advances of the wrong men, the men who wanted to suck from me the things that were useful to them, leaving behind only my shell, my carapace.

I pulled a chair into the kitchen to watch Jason at the stove. He had brought bone marrow, arborio rice, the succulent and thrilling and meaty parts of things that he knew I'd appreciate. He poured stock into the rice and stirred and stirred, his body making a rhythm in my tiny kitchen. He told me that the relationship with his girlfriend was waning. It was almost over, he said. It was a dying animal.

"Can you stay tonight?" I asked. He had been over a handful of times, though never for dinner. And he had never stayed the night. It had felt as if I had only had him for seconds at a time, as if the moments were so brief that they barely existed.

"Not tonight," he said. "But soon." Another promise. Another poem. The food was a poem, too. We sat down in my living room, which was also my dining room. In the corner, I had tucked a Pennsylvania Dutch table, hewn in the early 1800s, the kitchen table of my childhood. You could squeeze four people around it, if you were mindful of the giant red couch.

I looked at his face in the dim light of my apartment, his pointed chin, his red-tinged hair, his freckles. He was tall and thin and not conventionally handsome, and I had tried really hard not to end up here, over a bowl of risotto. The bone marrow was right on top, soft and pliant, the best part—the most tender—picked out for me to see.

At Sea Grill, there was a woman we called the Ice Queen. Every day, she showed up on the ice, without fail, dressed in lace and Lycra and thick nude tights. She did axels and lutzes and sophisticated turns in the center of the rink. Rockefeller had once been my home rink, too. My father had taken me to skate there almost every weekend in winter. It was a small and manageable oval, and one that I had loved in the same way that I had loved everything in Midtown, because everything in Midtown was over-the-top. The Rockefeller rink, where my father, in black figure skates, took my hands and skated backward toward the glass windows, was, even in the 1980s, a destination for tourists from all over the world. When we lived in Brooklyn, we took the train in to skate and to marvel at the tree and the white angels.

Now it was the Ice Queen's turn, this time for a daily supplication on the ice. She came, she saw, and she conquered, fully visible to the servers and diners of the dining room. Dressed always in powder blue, she resembled a Disney princess, twirling around in a loop until the Zamboni called all skaters off. At first, I expected her. Eventually, I looked forward to her, to the rise and fall of her stockinged legs, to the streaks she cut on the fresh ice. She was like a little toy, wound up and set apace, a point of interest so divergent from the same lemon-yellow wine that every table ordered, the same conversations, the same watery service, a repetition, a boring dance.

I had grown bored, too, of my dance with Jason. If he was leaving his girlfriend, it was certainly hard to make heads or tails of it. During the break between shifts, I began joining him across the street at Morrell, where I came equipped with a copy of the *New York Times* crossword puzzle. There, we charged through the answers together, even on the harder days, even on Fridays. He rested his chin on my shoulder, looking at the answers with a shared comfort that old couples enjoy. Jason wasn't the marrying type, he assured me. He just didn't believe in it. He never wanted to have children, either, and when I thought of my life, in the long, drawn-out version, that was a wrinkle.

"You'll never marry?" I asked.

"I don't think so," he said.

"And you never want kids?"

"I definitely don't."

Still, I believed that our love story could figure itself out, that the connection we shared could overcome whatever differences lay before us. Every day, we met at Morrell for crosswords and wine. The Ice Queen skated and we drank wine at the bar in the cold afternoons before service. Jason worked fewer and fewer nights, the fortunate recipient of the union's best shifts. He could cherry-pick the schedule, leave me, the sommelier and junior manager, with the lonely Monday nights, the glaze-eyed tourists, the dinners alone at the bar after service: a tuna tartare with a spray of tobiko atop it, popping in the mouth like tiny firecrackers.

I often think of what happens to an addict when the addiction becomes advanced. At first, it's a rush. It's just so much fun. But then, after a while, it becomes drudgery. By the time

I had landed myself at the Sea Grill, I was fully enmeshed in my restaurant addiction. I wasn't sure where else to turn for work. I hated my job, but what other work was there for me? And so every day, I fed my addiction to survive, selling bottles, doing the things I knew how to do. *Do you prefer your Chardonnay buttery, like toast?*

Nothing was ever enough. Each night after service, Jason secreted me away to the basement for a clandestine embrace before heading back to Brooklyn to his other life, his real life. I wondered if I was operating under the Carrie Fisher–esque cognitive dissonance demonstrated in *When Harry Met Sally.* "He's never going to leave her." ("No one thinks he's ever going to leave her," Meg Ryan retorts, in a later conversation about the same man.) I did think that Jason was going to leave her, though. I believed him when he said that he was unhappy, that they had been growing apart. It was my own delusion. I needed to believe him.

If I had fallen in love with wine because it had ignited in me a passion for learning, I had forgotten about that by now, trapped in the hell of one of the world's greatest tourist attractions, where every table wanted to tell me about their dreams of the biggest, creamiest, most buttery Chardonnay. They wouldn't spring for a bottle of Kistler—too spendy—but did I have anything in the $10-a-glass range? The Sea Grill didn't need a sommelier; they needed a maid to clean up after the atrocity of tourist dinner service. They needed a robot. I wasn't suited to the task. I wanted to fly through the dining room, the way I had at BLT, high on adrenaline. I wanted the rush of picking a guest's brain. *I like something fruity* could be translated to *full-bodied, rich, ripe.* We had language for that, as sommeliers. Fruity did not mean sweet. I liked using the powers of deduction to reduce a person's likes and dislikes down to a series of bottles in just a few minutes—I only ever had a few minutes. I liked the subtlety of talking about money without talking about money. I even liked the handshake that every so often contained a $100 bill, the swap off agreement between guest and professional, service rendered.

None of that was here, in this glass-walled prison, where my daily entertainment vacillated between the Ice Queen and my part-time boyfriend. It was my ennui—my situational boredom—that contributed to my obsession with my objectively nonexistent relationship. At work, I had nothing to look forward to, and so there was the quick clip of the crossword-puzzle afternoons at the wine bar, which seemed like a life, even though it really wasn't. I had to sink into that delusion to get away from the larger truth: that work was a joke, that I didn't belong at the Sea Grill any more than I had belonged anywhere else.

And it was, I see now, a complete and total delusion. I tricked myself into thinking that our affair was more than an affair because we were living it out in the open. We weren't being so secretive after all, I rationalized to myself. A person who has everything to hide tries harder to conceal it. But

Jason, taking the pen from my hand, holding my fingers for a beat too long, sipping from my glass to compare notes on wine, didn't seem to care about what anyone else was thinking. So how could I harbor any real doubts?

"I want to stay over tonight," Jason finally said one afternoon. After one month, two months, three—who could keep track?—he was finally making a decision. He was finally choosing me. The holidays were approaching and I felt better than ever about our relationship, which I had started talking about to people outside of work. Sure, Jason was never available to come out with me to any bars, and, sure, he may have been my absentee plus-one, but he was, as I put it, my *boyfriend.* We were just waiting, I thought, for the time to avail itself. We were just waiting for the right moment, for the seam in the universe to open up, for the complications to become less complicated. We were just waiting. But mostly I was just waiting, as Jason continued to live the life that he had always lived, perhaps with a few more added wrinkles.

The restaurant was intolerably busy. Guests from all over the world were arriving in droves, coming to visit Rockefeller Center even before the tree arrived. I was a wound-up toy, given my marching orders as soon as the restaurant opened each afternoon: open bottles, pour bottles, deliver glasses to tables, do not stop until the restaurant stops, rinse, repeat.

"Don't eat that," a sous-chef named Pat called to me,

catching me eating the olive bread behind the dish pit. "It will make you fat." I was on my feet for the better part of 12 hours a day and running into work every other day—five miles across the bridge from Queens. I was small, a size 2, in a suit that compressed every part of my body.

"I think I'm pretty small," I called back.

"I don't know about that," he said.

I stood in the kitchen, looking down at the bread. He had said the quiet part aloud.

I had struggled with my weight since putting on pounds in high school. Running had been a game of mental precision, but also a game of calorie counting. Could I compete with myself to keep the weight off? Could I make myself smaller and smaller until I was more likable, the way that was evidently so easy for other people?

I was intoxicated by the smell of bread coming from the kitchen, pleased by the chewy heels of it, the shriveled green olives tucked into the ends. I could have lived off of it, or I was already living off of it, shoving it into my mouth whenever I had the chance, eating almost nothing but bread and the occasional tartare at night. It was only bread, and I was hungry, and we were supposed to be people who loved food. But to be a woman who loved food was very different than to be a man who loved food. You were still supposed to care about restraint. You were supposed to love it, want it, understand it, obsess over it, talk about it constantly—but never really indulge in it. To indulge was to give up the last vestiges of control. To indulge was to slip from a size 0 to a size 2 to a size 4 to a size 6 and so on and so on.

The bread was chewy and delicious and necessary to my survival. Still, that day, I walked out without eating. I couldn't bear the thought of being watched like that, of having the sous-chef stare at me like I was a rabid animal on the hunt. Jason found me in the basement, back pressed to the wall.

"What happened?" he asked.

"Pat says not to eat the bread." I realized that it wasn't just Pat. It was an entire culture of Pats, of people who wanted me to look a certain way or act a certain way. Was there any winning in restaurants? Even in the most benign tourist trap—a place without a celebrity chef or a stealth general manager who was stealing Patrón by the case—I had come right up against the worst impulses of the industry. I wondered if there was a restaurant out there that didn't make people feel like shit. Every restaurant worker knows that the walk-in refrigerator is the place to go when you need to cry. But why, I thought to myself, do you have to work in a place where crying at work is considered a normal behavior? Why do we have to work like this at all?

Jason looked at me. "Well, fuck Pat, then," he said.

It wasn't much, but, in the moment, it was just enough, a salve to round out the rough edges of what I was feeling: abandonment, bruising, some kind of unidentified twisting pain. Restaurants, of course, were always forcing these mixed-up emotions on me, overwhelming me with too much, packing in too many feelings in too few hours. To assess your own value—to determine whether you were worthy by the metrics determined by a restaurant—you had to set aside everything else. You didn't have to be a good person to be good at restaurant work. You didn't have to be nice, or forgiving, or ethical, or kind. You only had to be willing to show up and dig into the work that was before you, even if that work was brutal and unfair and traumatic and mean. You did this all, much of the time, for a breathlessly small paycheck, given the number of hours you spent doing the actual work (I challenge both tipped and salaried restaurant workers to spend time calculating how much money they make per hour, after all is said and done). After this, to know that even something as simple as eating a piece of bread could be met with derision was almost more than a person could bear.

In moments of trauma—surely restaurants are nothing but a collection of these—it's not surprising that even small offerings of kindness can generate overly inflated reactions instead of equal and opposite reactions. The solidarity of two people in a kitchen felt like protection, and it was protection I needed, and so it was hard not to love Jason in moments like this. He pulled me up from the floor and into his arms. That's when he promised he would come over. He would stay. He promised that he would stay. I was not Carrie Fisher, my own suspicions be damned.

He did spend the night. I can't remember if we watched *Annie Hall* on my old VCR—the one I'd dragged from college to grad school and then back to New York—on some earlier evening or on the momentous evening when he didn't have to go home, the night when he came and simply did not leave. I do remember his supine figure, outlined in darkness, head on the pillow, looking up at the ceiling, at the crown molding, at my old walls. I had lived in the apartment for two years by then, since June of 2005, the month after graduating from my MFA program at Emerson. My stepmother had brought a box of kosher salt and a loaf of sliced rye, and I had forgotten about the bread for weeks. By the time I went to retrieve it, the loaf had turned seafoam green with sprouted mold. That was how often I had opened my own cabinets. That was how often I had treated my own home like a home.

I didn't know what Jason's Williamsburg apartment looked like on the inside; if it was tidy or a mess, if it had old bones and a soul like mine or if it was part of some slap-dash new-build that brought people in need of homes to their high-rent destinations in the mid-2000s. All I knew was that there was a puffy, large tabby cat, not at all the animal that I pictured when I pictured the home of my own dreams.

In the settling darkness, where I could see particles of dust rising and holding in the air, I wanted to freeze time. I wanted to take a picture. I wanted to memorize the way the room just stayed there, the light unmoving, save for a ceaseless fluorescent bar light that crept in through the bamboo blinds that my father had installed above the air conditioner, which I ran even in January, necessary to combat the old hissing radiator heat.

"Why are you here tonight?" I asked. I shouldn't have asked. I could have just let it go. Jason was here. He was next to me. I could see the rising and falling of his chest, and he was a real person, and this was real. That was what I had to keep telling myself, through the Ice Queen days, as I dragged myself to work a job that I loathed. The reward was Jason, a person just out of reach—but real. I could grant myself that.

For a second, he said nothing. He raised his hands high above his head, then used them as a makeshift pillow. He didn't look at me. "She's out of town," he said.

"For how long?"

"A week."

This was news to me. When we had left work that night, he had surprised me by letting me know that he would be coming over to stay. But the details had been murky. I hadn't wanted to ask about his girlfriend, whose name I hated to use, for fear that it would conjure a real person, a living, breathing human being in a parallel life in a parallel borough. I preferred to think of her as an incomplete sketch, a person who didn't fit together with Jason as neatly as I did. For all I knew, she hated his cooking, or drank cheap wine, or complained about the smell of cigarettes. In his brief mentions of her, he drew a picture of a relationship without sex, a friendship that had once had a strong center that was eroding over time. It was natural, he said. Even the longest and strongest things can start to fall apart. I thought of my own parents' marriage, which had ended in a movie theater, of all places, during a screening of the movie *Reds*, the three-hour 1981 love story about the Russian October Revolution. My parents had met at 18 and were married at 20 and 21, just before their senior year of college. Did their fatal flaw lie in their youth? Had the marriage cracked from the inside out?

Jason had met his girlfriend in Georgia, but I had been wrong about them. It wasn't a crumbling relationship. There would be no breakup in a darkened movie theater, no long-winded denouement.

"I guess I don't know what that means," I told him, suddenly understanding everything. My body started to feel sour. This wasn't the way it was supposed to go.

"It doesn't mean anything. It just is what it is."

I sat up straight. It did mean something. It meant that, on any other ordinary night, under ordinary circumstances, Jason Wagner would not be here, in my apartment, in my bed. He would be at home, with his girlfriend and his tabby cat, in the place where he belonged in the world, in the place he returned to when service was over. There was the Ice Queen, and then there was the life in Brooklyn, and I was just an accident in between, a misrouted subway stop in the wrong direction.

"Where does she think you are right now?" I asked.

"Probably home," he said. He wasn't looking at me. He didn't want to have this conversation. He wanted me to stop.

I wanted to stop, but there was a propeller inside of me, a force beyond my control. *An unstoppable force, an immovable object.* My father had once described my mother and me this way, but I couldn't remember which of us was which. Was I the object? The force? I felt like both, tied into one.

"If she were home right now, and it were this late, and you weren't there, what would she do?" I needed to know all of it, the excavation of their relationship, the truth laid before me like bones.

"Check the hospitals," he said. He did not miss a beat.

It wasn't over, then. Far from it. Somewhere, his speech pathologist girlfriend was traveling for work and imagining him safely at home. His disappearance would be so unusual—so dire, even—that she would have found herself driving around to Brooklyn's hospitals, scrambling around the wards of the weak, wounded, sick, and dying, in search of her love. He would never have put her through that, he was intimating. He would never have broken the code of their relationship, the holy agreement: to show up, to come home, to live this patched-together life.

He was never going to leave her. I knew that now, for sure.

My family had Thanksgiving without me. I worked the floor in a rigorous and unending double. No time for olive bread. No time to sit and think about the creeping pain leveling my calves and feet. Jason had worked at the Sea Grill for long enough to have priority when it came to major holidays and

I imagined him at home with his girlfriend and cat and a decanter full of the richest Barolo he could find, maybe a 2001 Borgogno that turned red-brown and that smelled like hot pavement in August. In my most vibrant imagination, they were carving a brown lacquered turkey in a quiet neighborhood apartment and listening to the November wind beat the trees back. His girlfriend had jet-black hair and short, close-cropped bangs and I was sure that no one who saw them on the street could have suspected what I knew about them, which was that a weed was growing in between, planted by accident, planted in a flimsy copy of Neruda's old poems. You could cut it back over and over again, but it was too late; it had already taken root.

In Massachusetts, my mother made the 30-pound turkey without my help. My uncles and cousins and aunts and grandmother and sister and brother sat down to eat the stuffing that only came out once a year, the kind that my mom insisted on making inside the bird—better-tasting, she swore. The key was turkey drippings and homemade stock and white button mushrooms sautéed in butter and Bell's poultry seasoning and a handful of oatmeal at the end to bind it all.

On Christmas, I woke up to an empty New York City. I stopped into the Apple Store on Fifth Avenue, a place that never closed, to buy a last-minute present. I went to work. Jason wasn't there, and so it was me and a million tourists. Everyone was with family. People often say that New York is a lonely city, despite its population. I never found it particularly lonely, except over those holidays, serving strangers, while my family ate in other cities, while my boyfriend ate with his girlfriend. Was I really going to sit around for every Christmas for the rest of my life, waiting on tourists and waiting for an ill-behaved man to come around?

Not long after the holidays, Jason booked a trip to Chicago with his girlfriend. He was taking her, he told me, to eat at Alinea, Grant Achatz's critically acclaimed restaurant where dinner often ended with a green apple cotton candy balloon. It was an obligation, he wanted me to know. He had to do it. It was for her birthday.

By then, I had stopped believing in fairy tales. Now that the holidays were over, the Ice Queen came to skate less and less. When Jason came back, I could see that something had changed.

"Did you have sex with her?" I asked. I don't know why I asked him this. She was his girlfriend. But I felt that I had a right to know.

He looked at the floor. "I did," he said. "We've been together for a really long time. It's complicated."

It wasn't really complicated to me, though it had become complicated. Caught up in the fervor of my high-paced workplace, I had been worn down. I had capitulated to my own worst impulses. I had been stupid. I had been duped.

There wasn't much to say after that. I tried to hold on for a while, grasping desperately at what I thought we had built together. My job was a moment of stagnation, a rotting away. I was hopeless and helpless and my relationship with Jason had been a respite from the reality of that. With Jason's departure from my life, I had to come face-to-face with the truth of the matter: Restaurants were beginning to tear me limb from limb. I wasn't sure how much more of them I could take.

I also left the Sea Grill with the feeling that I had been no more than a pawn in someone else's career chess game. During those afternoons at Morrell, when I was busy falling in love, it turned out that Jason was only busy furthering his career. He had been studying for his entry-level sommelier exams, with my help, and had used my name to increase his stature in the industry. I had been happy to offer recommendations on his behalf, but I had been less happy to learn that he had lied about his experience in public forums, claiming to have worked as a sommelier for long before even I had formally trained in wine. A few years after I left the Sea Grill, he would end up named one of the country's top sommeliers by *Food & Wine* magazine, though the magazine would go on to un-name him after he switched jobs midyear.

The girlfriend, of course, was no short-term fling. Jason married her and the two had a son. He had never wanted to get married, or he had never wanted to get married to me. He had never wanted kids, or that was just one more lie he told to get near me when it was convenient. What truths had he told in our time together? What distinguished fact from fiction?

In 2020, right before the start of the pandemic, Jason was let go from his position of wine director at Union Square Cafe after he was caught—I was told by colleagues—having sex with a sommelier in the wine cellar, on camera, during Friday night service. When I heard it, I sat down at my desk and stared out through the French doors of my kitchen. It hadn't been my fault, although I had truly believed that I was to blame. I had carried the shame of him with me for over a decade at that point, part of my litany of restaurant failures. Here was just another: an affair, my poor judgment, my silly emotional incongruity. But it was Jason who had been the predator, setting his sights on me, recognizing my vulnerability, sinking teeth into me from the very beginning. He had hunted me, trapped me, used me, and tossed me away, and all that time I had thought that I was to blame for my dependence on him. Rising through the ranks at restaurant after restaurant—repeating this act with who knows how many other women—Jason stole from me something that I could not get back.

I had never been allowed to enjoy, during my time at the Sea Grill, a full loaf of the olive bread. Only the stale and unused pieces—the ones too ugly to be served to guests—were the ones we could take. Only those would go unnoticed. But I see now that I deserved far more than the discards. I deserved more than secondhand boyfriends and secondhand bread. I deserved a plate all to myself, warm from the oven, studded with the plumpest, greenest olives available, sliced thick, with a slick of butter on the side, served only for me, nourishment for one.

*   *   *

Green-Olive Dutch-Oven Bread

Serves 8 to 10; makes a 1½-pound loaf

3⅓ cups (400 grams) all-purpose flour,
   plus more for dusting
¼ teaspoon instant yeast
2 teaspoons kosher salt
1 cup (180 grams) coarsely chopped pitted
   Castelvetrano olives
1½ cups (390 grams) room-temperature water
High-quality salted butter, for serving

Combine the flour, yeast, and salt in a mixing bowl. Use a spatula or wooden spoon to gently stir in the olives until evenly coated. Add the water and stir until the ingredients are well combined (the dough will be wet and extremely sticky). Cover the bowl with plastic wrap and let rest in a draft-free spot at room temperature until dotted with bubbles on top, 12 to 19 hours.

Lightly flour a work surface. Turn the rested dough out onto the work surface. Dust the top with more flour and fold the dough over on itself (a bench scraper is helpful here).

Cover the dough with plastic wrap or a slightly damp kitchen towel and let it rest for 20 minutes.

Shape the dough into a ball using a small amount of flour—just enough to prevent the dough from sticking. Coat one side of a dish towel with flour and use the floured side to cover the dough; allow it to rise in a draft-free spot at room temperature for another 2 hours. The dough should double in size and will not spring back when pressed with a finger.

When the dough has rested for 1½ hours, place a lidded 6- to 8-quart Dutch oven in the oven and preheat to 450°F. When the dough has fully risen (at 2 hours), carefully move the Dutch oven to the stovetop (off the heat) and grease its interior with cooking oil spray. Use a pastry brush to remove any excess flour from the dough, then quickly turn the dough into the hot Dutch oven.

Cover with the lid, return the pot to the oven, and bake for 30 minutes. Remove the lid and bake for another 15 to 30 minutes, until the loaf has developed a rich caramel crust and the internal temperature of the bread registers at least 190°F on an instant-read thermometer.

Transfer the pot to a wire rack to cool for 10 minutes. Take out the bread and let it cool completely on the rack. Serve at room temperature, alongside your high-quality salted butter.

7 | CHEF-FUCKER

The party never ended at Momofuku. "Turn the music *UP,*" David Chang liked to say when he walked into the dining room at Momofuku Ssäm Bar, on Second Avenue near East 13th Street. The sound system was no more than an original generation iPod, cycling Dave's hand-picked mixes through rudimentary speakers. Ssäm Bar opened in 2006, two years before I was hired to take over the beverage program for three restaurants: Momofuku Noodle Bar, Momofuku Ssäm Bar, and the newest outpost, Momofuku Ko, a 12-seat fine dining restaurant on First Avenue with a prix-fixe, multicourse menu and an impossible-to-crack reservation system.

Could I get you a table at Ko? Actually, I could. Sort of. But I wasn't supposed to tell you about it. Every morning, the bloggers and the food obsessives went online exactly at

10 a.m. to see about reservations for the next week. It was a who-can-click-fastest game, a matrix that favored the slick-thumbed. The people who won out were often the same people who fared well at beating the scalpers when Springsteen tickets went on sale. You had to be in your seat at a computer at a minute or so before the clock struck 10, had to click the button, and if grace favored you, if the gods of the reservation system rained down upon you, maybe—just maybe—you could get yourself one of those coveted seats that everyone in New York *just had to have*, the year's answer to the Birkin bag, a luxury accessory all its own.

Of course, I knew what millions of New Yorkers did not, which was that, like every other restaurant in history, Ko had its share of cancellations. We knew about these cancellations on the floor, which is how I was able to tip off the occasional friend or industry insider to an open seat, should they happen to be in the area. My friends who had expressed interest in dining at the Hottest Restaurant in the City were all noted in my BlackBerry, my own personal wait list. If you lived within walking distance of the East Village, you just might happen to find yourself sitting at Ko on a given night, no reservation required.

Sometimes, I'd text a friend and it just wouldn't work. New York City's vast landscape would make it impossible. They'd be in Brooklyn. They'd be at dinner somewhere else. They'd be uptown, and it would take way too long to get down to the East Village. Fair enough. One night, though, the stars aligned. A cancellation had opened up two prime seats in the middle of service, a juicy experience for two people who were willing to drop everything and show up immediately, provided they could put on the kind of act that the entire charade required. I knew just who to text.

"If you can get here in the next 20 minutes and just pretend you're checking on availability, it's yours," I said to my friend André Mack by text message. Mack was once the renowned sommelier at Thomas Keller's Per Se. These days, he co-owns several Brooklyn restaurants, including Kingfisher, Mockingbird Taco, and & Sons Ham Bar. A few minutes after my text, he showed up at the door with a very pregnant Phoebe Damrosch, his wife and also the author of a book about the inner workings of waiting tables at a four-star restaurant in the early 2000s: *Service Included*. With her affable sway—belly out *to here*—you never would have recognized dear Phoebe as the girl in the gray and black uniform from the pin-drop-quiet dining room in the Time Warner Center.

André and Phoebe stood at the door to Ko. There was no host stand; the restaurant was simply too small to accommodate one. Were there any seats available, they wanted to know? What a lucky night, I told them. Two seats had *just* opened up. I ushered them in to the end of the bar, where luck continued: they had just scored the most difficult-to-obtain reservation in all of New York, and no one was any the wiser.

The servers and I, it should be known, regularly offered this known-only-to-us service—a text-message wait list—if a seat happened to open up at Ko. The ruse was important. It may even have been essential to the context of the restaurant. We had to make sure that Ko appeared full at all times, because the desirability of Ko hinged upon the inability of patrons to be able to get a seat. Should a diner find herself next to an empty seat, the façade would crumble; then it might just be an ordinary restaurant, with an extraordinarily moneyed crowd, palling around the East Village on a Tuesday night, say, willing to blow way too much cash on a multicourse meal. Yes, the fluke draped in poppy seeds, splayed delicately with chopsticks by Peter Serpico himself, was good. But was it good enough to keep you at your computer every single morning at 10 a.m. for the rest of your life? I had my doubts. André and Phoebe fell for Ko, it seemed. The restaurant, I had to admit, could be intoxicating. At the end of dinner, they walked out and winked.

I wasn't always at Ko, minding the door, or playing Tetris with the tiny beverage refrigerator that housed the minuscule wine selection that I sold to the restaurant's well-heeled crowd. As beverage director, I was required to split my time among the floors of the different restaurants, but Noodle Bar rarely needed my attention, since it was the most casual venue with very little wine service. Some nights, then, you could find me roaming the floor at Ssäm, trying to unload the magnum of Screaming Eagle that I had unwisely put on the wine list and aimed to pawn off on a large party for just under $10,000. Other nights, you could find me at Ko, where I was the model of fine dining gentility, serving everyone in the elite dining class and distributing mise-en-place with the appropriate decorum.

I preferred the grittiness of Ssäm to the buttoned-up perfectionism of Ko. At Ssäm, we could slam sake glasses full of OB beer, the South Korean answer to Bud Light. At Ssäm, we could order a plate of steamed pork buns with their rich belly, crunch of salted cucumber pickle, and swipe of candied hoisin at the end of a grueling evening. At Ssäm, we could dance across the dining room. When Ira Glass, the geeky, black glasses–donning NPR host came into the bar at Ssäm, I said, without missing a beat, "You and the Little Mermaid can *both* go fuck yourselves!" referencing an iconic episode of *This American Life;* thankfully, he laughed instead of walking out. If you want to know what it feels like to be a lightbulb that has just been plugged in, work in a restaurant. If you want to know what it feels like to be a lightbulb that has just been replaced with higher wattage, go back in time and work at Ssäm Bar in 2008. This was joy, it was power, it was information, it was sex, it was buzz, it was a feeling so distinct and alive that I couldn't help wanting it again and again. Which is why, I suppose, I looked forward to that time of day when the sun sank behind the buildings on the East Side, and the cadence changed in the dining room, and everyone started to get amped up.

I had a boyfriend at Ssäm, kind of. He was the same age as I was, and he had worked at the restaurant longer. He was an industry lifer, the kind of person who starts in restaurants and falls in love—much as I had—with the late nights and the camaraderie. After service, when no one was watching, we caught a cab and headed over the Queensboro Bridge together, then smoked Parliament Lights out the window of my apartment into the airshaft until the sun played patterns on the pre-war millwork. He had the sturdy composition of a college soccer player, and he was a die-hard Yankees fan, something we had in common—perhaps the only thing. He didn't want to talk about politics or books. He didn't want to worry about the future the way that I did. His presence of mind was the present. He lived in the Bronx, I was convinced, to be closer to the stadium, and when he left in the mornings, always at first full light, it was as if the shame of day had reminded him that we were two different people.

"See ya," he'd say, grabbing his portfolio bag and heading to the subway, maybe taking a cigarette for the road.

It was a flat, unsatisfying relationship, the kind that restaurants deliver with certainty. I never knew when I would see my waiter boyfriend again, except for when the stars of our shifts would align. After work, I could cruise by the bar we often closed down and peek in through the red-curtained windows to see if he was sitting there, drink in hand.

Sometimes, I could make out his figure, shadowy, slightly hunched over, a beer bottle in front of him, a shot in front of him, too. He was everyone's best friend and, in public, he was mine, too, though he wanted our Queens affair to remain private. No one needed to know about our trips across the glittering, early morning East River, where each of us would stare silently from separate windows of the cab, looking out onto the city and its infinite stillness, during those hours when nothing was either awake or asleep. A milky moon beating down on the water, a black liquid river, two people crossing from one borough into the next and full of twentysomething indecision: at the time, to me, that felt like love.

I was not brave enough to understand that a lack of relationship defined my relationship, that the same murkiness surrounding all aspects of restaurant life made my love life equally impossible. But, in a sense, what I had with my waiter was, ironically, stability and comfort, particularly in the wake of my other relationship, which was the one I was in with my boss, David Chang. Even in our impetuous, late-night trysts, there was some gasping for air. That waiter and I, we needed each other, and I knew that we would come together again and again, rolling around until one of us had had enough. It was secure in a way that my work relationship was not. That relationship was all fire and smoke and chemical imbalance. With my waiter lover, temperate indifference was a reliable circumstance. But with Dave (or David, or Chang; alternating names, alternating moods), a bomb was always about to go off, or a bomb had always just gone off, or you were always ducking for cover from the shrapnel. His temper was riotous, his outbursts contagious. The kitchen and dining room could shake with the force of his wrath. The first time I heard him threaten a sous-chef, I did not, sadly, head immediately for the door. I did not email the de facto head of human relations, EunJean Song. I also didn't cower in fear. Instead, I ignored Chang's anger, digested it, and moved on with my night.

He was a chef, and I had heard other chefs explode, and his first explosion probably seemed a lot like other explosions that I had witnessed. It was only later, once I put together the pieces of what I had witnessed—how Chang preferred the performance of anger, how he targeted the staff members that he felt were weaker or less cool, how he fostered a culture of cliquishness that I hadn't felt since high school—that I realized that I may have been rationalizing his behavior during my time at his restaurants. If his lava-hot anger felt par for the course in mid-2000s restaurants, that was a reflection of restaurants and their chefs, and not of whether or not Dave was a "normal" part of them.

Everyone who worked at Momofuku had a chance to experience the tidal wave of Chang's emotions. One day it could be directed at someone else, the next fiercely at you. When the wave crested, it was always with an audience, intended, I always believed, to humiliate. The humiliation was worse than any real threat of harm or violence. For me, it felt familiar, to be yelled at by someone who was my superior. It reminded me of home, where two things could be true at once, where it was possible to be both terrified and in need of acceptance, envelopment, and even love. If the smell of cubes of pork hitting a wok could bring me back to the early 1990s, to a Massachusetts kitchen where my sometimes-recalcitrant stepfather could redeem himself with the fragrance of food from a place that he had visited in the Air Force, Chang's food could be equally transportive. Or perhaps it wasn't transportive so much as it was a tendon, a living tissue connecting us, two people, one ordinary (me), one extraordinary (him), tethered by rice cakes in crimson gochujang; a pork blade steak sliced into long pink ribbons; sweetbreads cooked on the plancha and served with a fiery nuoc cham.

Every time that Chang screamed—at me, at others—I dove headlong into something delicious afterward to forget about the things that he had said. *Who the fuck do you think you are? I will fucking scalp you. I will murder your family. You are bad at your job. The back-of-the-house has more talent.* I could forget these things, it turned out, the same way I could forget a lot of things, by driving myself harder, by convincing myself that the passion for the work and the passion for the food were reason enough to excuse the inexcusable. I could forget, because my brain and my body had been trained, from years and years and years of it, to walk into the fire of trauma and walk out again, burned but not broken—or so I chose to believe at the time. You can imagine yourself one way, it turns out, before understanding that it is not at all true, before understanding the depths of your own despair.

We knew what was coming. If you open a restaurant in New York, you always know what is coming. You invite the critic with a mixture of nervous anticipation and wrath. What right, after all, does this interloper—this *non-restaurant person*—have to pass judgment on your place of business? Even a lowly server, hardly responsible for the way food tastes or looks, feels protective of the restaurant when it comes time for the review. There is a sacred battle between critic and server, long played out in the meaty belly of restaurants. One eats, the other watches in desperation. Will this person destroy careers, suck not only fat from bones but also lifeblood from a place of employment? At a place like Ko, where reservations were monitored with precision, we could see every single face walk in our door, and so we knew the minute that Frank Bruni, food critic for the *New York Times*, walked in to seal our fate.

"Best of luck. Be strong. Be forewarned." Bruni would go on to write these three sentences in the second paragraph of his May 7, 2008, review of Momofuku Ko. If Bruni's words read like an indictment, they were not. The review, which was published online the night before, on Tuesday, May 6, in the fiery rush of service, had awarded the restaurant an unlikely three stars. Restaurants like Ko didn't get three stars. Even Bruni, in his review, conceded as much. "At

Ko, you straddle a backless stool," he wrote. The restaurant was immune to the creature comforts historically extended to patrons of three-star restaurants: tablecloths, plush banquettes, even hard liquor, owing to a licensing issue.

We knew Bruni was coming. Near the service station, we kept a plastic binder filled with photographs of *important media*. Steve Plotnicki, who had exploited Black rap artists and then started a blog called *Opinionated About Dining* with his plunderings; Adam Platt, the critic from *New York* magazine; Dana Cowin, then editor in chief of *Food & Wine;* Kate Krader, the restaurant editor from the same magazine, who nipped at Dave Chang's heels like a dog in heat; Pete Wells, known, then, for his "Cooking With Dexter" column in the *New York Times Magazine;* and then, of course, the Big Kahuna, the king of food media himself, Frank Bruni, the former Rome bureau chief who became the newspaper's food critic in 2004.

Like the other food personalities who had come in—Gael Greene, most notably, who had arrived with a young gentleman guest, Tom Dobrowski, and had called me a gorgon in an *Insatiable Critic* piece that ran just one day before the *Times* review—Bruni's reservation was made under a pseudonym. He ate at the restaurant once, about a month before he reviewed us and only a month after I had accepted the position of beverage director. That night, I was working double time. My boss, Cory Lane, had left to go to the soft opening of Jason and Joe Denton's Bar Milano on 24th and

Third. "Email me if absolutely anything happens," he said. We probably weren't expecting the worst.

Something did happen, though. Bruni came in, and before I had a chance to let Cory know, Dave was screaming his head off. "Where the *fuck* is Cory?" he wanted to know. Dave started punching numbers into his BlackBerry. I started punching numbers into mine. Cory didn't appear, and a thick mist settled on the kitchen, a feeling of dread, a feeling of anger, Chang's mood palpably worse. You could feel the weight of Chang when he was there, the burden of him. You were governed by his emotional state. If he was happy, you were permitted to feel joy. If he was wrathful, peace be with you, dear friend. You were in for the most terrible ride of your life.

Ludicrously, even though I was at the restaurant and Cory was, presumably, sitting at the glossy Bar Milano, some 10 blocks uptown, getting blitzed, I got an email back, at 10:47 p.m. Subject line: *Re: Bruni is at ko.* Text: *Can you make sure all the wine is spot on.* Not even any punctuation. Fuck Cory, who had promised that he would rush back in an emergency. Considering the color of Dave's face, this certainly felt like an emergency to me. I made sure that Bruni's wine—and every other beverage that touched his lips—was spot on. So spot on was my wine service, in fact, that he wrote about it in the *New York Times.* My pairing of Budweiser with soft-shell crab? It brought out a "sense of mischief," Bruni wrote. Of all the pairings that I have poured in all of the restaurants that I have worked in, no other one has fully combined my intellectual understanding of food and wine with my disruptive streak. And Bruni got it.

He grinned at me—just a soft side-eye—as I presented the bottle, not unlike the way I would have presented even the most expensive bottle of ace vintage Lafite. I tipped it back toward my forearm so that he could examine its red and white label and then held it from the butt of the bottle and poured into the sake glass that we used for tastings, wiping the lip with a serviette used for wine service. Twist, wipe, lift. There's an arm movement associated with pouring wine that feels like second nature once you've been doing it long enough. It's meant to ensure that nothing spills on the guest, but it's also just a mannerly flourish, a touch of fine dining gravitas. When I did it with the bottle of Bud, it was meant to be tongue-in-cheek. Here you are, after all, paying hundreds for a dinner, born of the sweat and tears and free labor of stagiaires, and what do you get? Budweiser. I loved the theater of it, and I loved that this place—this wild and crazy place—had let me get away with it.

As much as the culture was forgiving for the creative-minded, it was also conventional in terms of expectation. Cory, the general manager, was expected to be on property for a Very Important Critic appearance. That was a conventional way of thinking, as far as restaurants were concerned. Cory never did come back to the restaurant that night, and Chang, barking from the pass, covered from the chest down in a full white apron, remained the hue of a boiled lobster until well after the man who paid with a credit card under the name of John, or David, or Richard left the slight East Village restaurant. Only then did the chef wipe his brow and untie his whites and stumble into the back for a respite from the exhaustion of what was most certainly the crucial review of 2008.

As it turned out, not showing up on review night had gotten Cory into quite a bit of trouble. The next day, Drew Salmon, Momofuku's chief of operations, took the managers of all of David Chang's restaurants out for lunch at a ramen place that had just opened on Fourth Avenue between 9th and 10th. "We're here for research and development," he said as we filed in, representatives from Momofuku Ssäm Bar on Second Avenue, Momofuku Noodle Bar on First, and Momofuku Ko, right next door to Noodle.

Ippudo Daimyo, a ramen restaurant that began in Fukuoka, Japan, in 1985, is known for their tonkotsu ramen, a soup made from springy noodles and pork bone broth. The bones are cooked for so long that the soup itself appears milky. My entire relationship with ramen, until I walked into Ippudo, had been with the instant noodle packets of my youth—and with a brand in particular called Oodles of Noodles, which my parents bought for about 10 cents apiece. My stepfather, who had traveled the world in the Air Force, boiled them on the stove and cracked in a runny egg; that, to me, had been the pinnacle of unfamiliar comfort. My Jewish family ate chicken noodle soup, but not this, not soup thickened with egg.

Still, soup made from a packet with noodles rehydrated on the stove cannot prepare you for the bite of a noodle that has been made by hand, or for the taste of a broth that has been made from the deep marrow of bone and the hard boil of cartilage and trotter. We were there to appreciate a craft, as I saw it, and not to pilfer. Although, when I look back on it now, I wonder how much of what we did was camaraderie-aided theft. Dave, not Japanese, would go on to make ramen one of his signature dishes, even though you could go just blocks away and eat at Ippudo, sinking into the booths and falling deeply in love with the truth of it, which was that this is how it had always been made and that this is how it should always be made.

That day, we were not necessarily part of some scheme to steal industry secrets; for all I know, it was just a meal. Or Drew was just measuring, by the looks of glee as we sat steaming our faces over our bowls, how profitable it might be to become more ramen, less ambiguous noodle. But that wasn't why he had called us, after all. My broth was gray. It was the color of January. It was the color of thunderstorms. It tasted like pleasure. It tasted like someone had really cared. The noodles curled up and down in my mouth. A plate of fried chicken arrived, so crisp I thought I might break a tooth on the exterior. You can bite into chicken like that and think: *Why have I ever eaten it any other way?*

I wanted to evaporate into lunch, to live in the world of Ippudo Daimyo. (Of note: the DBA—a business's official operating name when they apply for a liquor license—for Ssäm Bar was Daimyo, a term that actually refers to Japan's old feudal system.) This was a meeting about a different daimyo, though, the Ssäm daimyo. Drew wanted to update us on our feudal overlord, Cory Lane.

"As many of you know, Bruni came into Ko last night," Drew said.

Everyone did, of course. It had been in the nightly manager log, a series of emails distributed at the end of the night among staff that lists the important happenings at each restaurant, from celebrity guest appearances to critic visits.

Drew cleared his throat. "Cory Lane is currently on leave for the next two weeks," he said. This was news to me. Up until this point, Cory had been the person I had answered to. He had taught me about the budgets, the vendor contacts, the Momofuku protocol. He had told me who to become friends with and who to avoid. Now I was all on my own, a new girl, just weeks into a new job, twisting in the wind.

I didn't have to ask why Cory was being put on unpaid administrative leave for two weeks; it had everything to do with the Bruni Event. When Cory had failed to show up for the review, Chang had been livid. That boiled lobster face was not just a symptom of the critic-in-the-house panic that every chef gets in the middle of a serious review. No. Chang had expected Cory, who was, by turns, his right-hand man and general manager of all things Momofuku, to *get his ass back* from 24th Street and manage the dining room.

Now, for two weeks, it would be only me, which meant that Ko, in particular, would be left with no real rules. My office, which was in the basement of Ssäm Bar, was where I would go to place wine orders for all three restaurants. During the day, I would walk between the three restaurants, conducting inventory and making sure that everyone had what they needed for service. At night, I would trade off between the two spots that most needed me—Ssäm and Ko. There, I would work as a floor sommelier, selling wine and pairing beverages.

"Does everyone understand the roles?" Drew asked. But it was only me, I felt, who had to adapt to this new reality. I was the one who would be walking back and forth and back again, the soles of my shoes practically worn through from the triangle between the three restaurants. I met with wine reps, I placed orders, I brought bottles up and down the stairs. I raced from one spot to the next to be where I needed to be in time for this meeting, that meeting, family meal, staff training. Two weeks was a very long time.

By the time Cory returned, I had already settled into a way of life at Momofuku, and so he pulled back on any kind of instruction. Mostly, he offered suggestions. Did I want to order this weird bottle of Favia wine? (I didn't, but it didn't really seem like a choice.) Did I want to switch my days off to

Tuesdays? (Not particularly.) At over 6 feet tall, Cory could hardly blend in, but he did try to stay out of my way. He busied himself by trying to look important, schmoozing with high-profile characters at the bar in the evenings and hiring wine nepo baby Christina Turley to join the Momofuku ranks, which really was an excuse to acquire hard-to-get allocated Turley wines, some of which mysteriously disappeared before making it to the wine list.

During the time between Bruni's visit and when his review was published, we remained one of New York's most popular restaurant groups. In the afternoon, when Ssäm opened for dinner, a modest line had already formed outside the restaurant door. The reservation system at Ko was making news over and over again, and we were serving so many elite and recognizable dining guests every night that we had basically stopped pretending that we didn't know who they were. Danny Meyer came in to sit at the counter at Ko. We were official, and we hadn't even landed in the *Times* yet.

And then, of course, we did land in the *Times*. At Ssäm Bar, where we served food until two in the morning, I was still working through a frightful pop when someone from the back-of-the-house refreshed a computer screen and there it was: three impressive stars, a holiday, a party, a celebration. Somehow, this group of Merry Pranksters had convinced the paper of record that we were serious. I had poured Budweiser from the bottle tableside, as if it were a bottle of Richebourg! Dave had frozen a torchon of foie gras and shaved it with a

Microplane over lychees and peanut brittle so that it looked like a hill of falling snow! We had operated without our general manager! The chopsticks rested on old wine corks! And somehow, in all of this chaos and weirdness and lack of finesse, Frank Bruni, food critic of the *New York Times,* had given us three stars!

To celebrate, everyone from the entire Momofuku entourage—servers and cooks and busboys—took cabs over to the Rusty Knot, which was owned by Quino Baca, a former Momofuku employee and a good friend of Dave's. Quino's wife, Nadia, a part-time actor with gigs on a few television shows of note, was also one of a handful of rotating servers who worked the floor in the evenings at Ko. She was slim and quiet with a bit of a mean streak that fit in with the Momofuku ethos. To fit in at Momofuku, after all, you couldn't be nice. You could pretend to be nice, but you couldn't actually mean it.

It was hard to know where I fit in when it came to this jigsaw puzzle of personalities. I wasn't mean, but I was a misfit. After work, I was happy to commiserate with the servers and creative personalities at the late-night bars. Even though I was upper management, I wasn't treated like a manager, and I wasn't included in the camaraderie extended to Dave's so-called Momo family. From the outside, it was a happy place to work, a communal place, where everyone pushed everyone else to be better. But inside, it felt competitive and exclusive, and, for me, unwelcoming. It was a workplace led by people who wanted you to believe that they had your best interests in mind, when really they wanted you to fail.

In no case was this truer than in the case of Christina Tosi who was, at the time, the redheaded genius who had been messing around in the kitchen at Ssäm Bar as Dave's pastry chef. Mostly, she amassed stockpiles of sugary treats and converted them into weird and hard-to-parse desserts, but one of them—corn flakes soaked in milk, which she translated into culinary speak, *an infusion*—became the backbone of her nascent empire. Cereal milk. It was like what was left behind in a little kid's breakfast bowl, the soggy underbelly of dishes left to rot in the sink. People went wild for the milk in all its permutations, moved, I guess, by the nostalgia. All at once, they were back in some 1980s-era kitchen, seated at a Formica counter, spooning wet corn flakes into their mouths. Cereal milk became the idea that launched Milk Bar, first no more than a tiny outpost across the street from Ssäm, on 13th Street between Second and Third.

But before Tosi was an eponymous household name, she was a pastry chef, prone to cozy gestures. At the Rusty Knot, she was already waiting inside, part of Dave's inner circle, first to arrive, last to leave. Dave trusted his friends, who were, in part, also his employees. Cory Lane may have pissed him off, but the two were still wrapped up in this thing together. Tosi had been with him from the start, just like Quino, who had left to pursue his own restaurant, sure, but was still part of the old Momo crew.

My work may have been called out in Bruni's review, but I would have been fooling myself if I thought that such a generous compliment was enough to bring me into the Momofuku fold. To roll with the big guns, the big guns had to tell you when they were ready for you. I sat down in a booth. It was well after midnight and the room was full of people.

Then, in some abstract gesture of conciliation—some gesture proving that, yes, I was ready to roll with the big guns—Dave slid into the booth, across from me. "Good work the other night," he said. It was the first time—and, in my memory, the last time—that he ever extended a compliment.

"Thanks," I said.

"We need a drink."

And then one came out, a ceramic bowl that was filled to the brim with cerulean liqueur. The drink was promptly set ablaze by one of the servers, and Dave and I received multicolored straws. Bar patrons cheered us on. "Drink, drink!" they roared. We drank until the cauldron was empty, and then beers arrived in their place.

Johnny Iuzzini walked in around then with a woman on his arm, which is when my memory turns sticky. The energy seemed to shift toward him, as if he were the sun. He had that kind of magnetism, but I could feel the night collapsing. I knew bad things were happening, but it was hard to know how bad. I had seen him come in and Christina Tosi had seen my face, some contortion, some revelation in my mouth or eyes. "Do you know him?" she asked.

It was a hard question to answer. What had been our relationship, actually? The correct answer—that we had worked together, and that he had once asked to place a pillowcase over my head—felt like the wrong one, in practically any setting, so I came up with a fudged response. We had sort of, kind of dated. I realized that also didn't fit, but it sounded better than the alternative—that I had only been sleeping with him.

"I used to date him," I said, knowing that it wasn't exactly the right language, that I wasn't being clear, but that being clear was not possible, like my tongue was too big in my mouth.

Christina had jolly eyes, the kind of eyes you want to trust, the kind of eyes that make a millionaire out of cakes and saccharine cookies.

"No, no, I get it," she said. "I completely get it."

A drink came my way, and, on its heels, a second. The bar began to feel dimmer, or brighter, or happier, or less happy, the way that a bar does when the drink number has escaped your notice. No one ordered food, though they should have. I began to feel, in the thickness of late evening, that teams had already been chosen, a chef with his longtime allies and me, a person with no team, out in the cold. I was not a celebrity, and I was definitely not a chef.

Johnny saw me out of the corner of his eye. I registered his displeasure. Christina whispered something in his ear. A girl left in tears. The outer edges of the evening began to become very smudged and hazy. No one knew about the pillowcase, but they certainly knew whatever version of the story that Johnny had told, and it looked less and less impressive by the 4 a.m. light of the Rusty Knot on the West Side Highway.

"That was Johnny Iuzzini's girlfriend," another person told me. "She didn't know that he cheated on her with you."

It had been news to me as well.

Outside, someone put me into a cab. I was swaying with the breeze, tipping over so far that I was worried I might crash into the pavement. It was a long ride back to Queens and by the time I made it to my pre-war apartment building and paid the driver, I had lost my keys. Standing outside in the chilled black night, I pounded on the doors until a stranger let me in.

"Who are you?" he said, blinking in the streetlamp.

"I live here," I said, hoping it was true.

When I woke up the next morning, I felt scratchy and wooly-eyed, as if someone had spread sandpaper across my corneas as I slept. I suffered the indignity of the train, its rumblings, its silent judgments. New York is an impersonal place, but in a moment of recognition, when you long to be truly alone with your indiscretions, the city is a mirror, an exacting reflection of every mistake you've ever made. In the dark tunnels of the snaking train, I saw the bags under my eyes staring back at me through scratched plastic windows. I saw my puffy face. I saw proof that one drink had led to more and more drinks and then to a sincere lapse in memory—brownout, blackout, who even knew? You could cheat time in your late teens and early 20s, but, at some point, those nights out catch up with you, and what I was looking at was hardly a ghost; what I was looking at was me. On the way to the train, I found my keys, tossed in the middle of the street; I supposed I had done that in a moment of recklessness, just thrown my own keys in the middle of 42nd Street in Astoria, frustrated with restaurants, frustrated with Johnny, frustrated with being lied to, mad that I had gotten so sloppy that someone had needed to put me in a cab. I had been lucky, both this time and other times, lucky enough to make it home without any real kind of trouble.

After that night at the Rusty Knot, I knew that I had been wrong about avoiding trouble. There was plenty of it in store for me at work.

At Ssäm Bar, I snuck in with a tall fountain soda and a pair of Prada sunglasses, but Drew was waiting for me in my office in the basement.

"I heard it was an exciting evening at the Rusty Knot," he said.

"Plenty to celebrate," I said, tossing my hobo bag—the one I had bought with my first-ever paycheck from BLT—onto a folding chair. Drew was sitting at my desk, at my computer, leaning back in my chair. I sat in the chair next to him, like a patient following a doctor's lead.

"So," he said, tipping back and forth in the chair, resting

his Converse All Stars on my paperwork, "I do have a question for you."

"Sure," I said.

"Are you a chef-fucker?" he asked. The words held in the air like Mylar balloons, aloft. Honestly, I didn't even know what a *chef-fucker* was, beyond the obvious. It wasn't a term people used, like *social climber*. No one I knew went out with the intention of *fucking chefs*. In restaurants, you just fucked people you worked with, which is like every other workplace on earth, except that it was probably a little more common in restaurants, where the hours are grim and the free time nonexistent. Who were you supposed to fuck, exactly, if not your coworkers, when you are working 15 hours a day and had only a single day off every week to yourself, and, on that one sacred day off, which probably falls smack in the middle of the week, when all of the regular people go to work at their regular jobs, you wake up at 11 a.m. and then take care of the shit that you can never manage to take care of on the six other days? How are you supposed to date *non-restaurant people*, when your unbalanced life has you spending every waking moment in a restaurant and filling your non-restaurant spaces with the upkeep of your life. If you were lucky, you had time to go to a gym, or visit a family member, or deposit a check at the bank during working hours. But date a person who didn't have the exact same insane schedule as you? Good fucking luck.

The fact that Drew had gone and made something up about me—that I was a chef-fucker, or whatever that was—was hardly the worst part, I thought. First of all, he was a nine-to-fiver. He had never worked actual restaurant hours, so what did he even know about the constraints of trying to be a human being in a world that was made for machines. Restaurants want your soul, but who can really survive the grind besides a Pacojet, or a Vitamix, or a Robot Coupe? Not an actual person, made from sinew and bone and blood, that was for sure. There was, too, all the work I had done that had not been in restaurants—all the studying, the learning, the stupid fucking internships in Congress and at *The New Yorker,* where I had dumped out Françoise Mouly's ashtray a million fucking times a day. This had all been pretty useless, it turned out. My whole life, I had been these other things: smart, funny, talented, loyal, acerbic, sarcastic, a little self-righteous, sure. But here, in a room designed to store wine bottles, at a place where I had been hired to run the beverage program for a major restaurant group, I was only a chef-fucker. Only that.

The rumor of my chef-fucking had not passed from bro to bro in some back-alley hand slap. It had passed to the director of operations to me, here in my basement office, where I was now forced to defend my own sex life. Was I a chef-fucker? I had fucked chefs, but I didn't think that my identity was any more that than it was anything else: autumn-lover, subway-rider, wearer-of-hooded-sweatshirts.

"You know, after I hired you, I got a call about you," Drew went on to say.

This was not the first time that I had heard about my blacklisting. It had now been exactly a year since I had left BLT Prime with my belongings in paper takeout bags, and the restaurant was still trailing me, still making calls to ruin my reputation. But it had not been BLT who had accused me of sleeping around this time. This time, I suspected, it had been Christina Tosi, the soon-to-be-world-famous pastry chef, and, as I was learning in the confines of the wine room-slash-office, a very close friend of one Johnny Iuzzini.

"That's good to know," I said.

"I hired you anyway."

On the day that Dave interviewed me, we had met a few blocks away, at a tiny Italian café. It was February, but we had sat outside, in the blistering cold, and Dave asked me a series of questions about work while staring down at the table. I had wondered, at the time, as I stared with equal discontent into a coffee—call it a latte, the kind of foamy and noncommittal drink I probably would have ordered back then—how a man who had been feared and adored and critically acclaimed and *all of those things* could be so abstractly impersonal with a stranger in person. He seemed sheepish, put off, I thought, by the idea of a midday coffee with a woman he didn't know. He knew nothing about wine, he conceded; that would be my program to run. He was quiet, and not at all tart or mean. Chang's wrath always arrived when there were other people around to witness it, because he did his best work when it was part of a larger

performance. I would come to see him as these dual personalities, twisting serpents coexisting in the same man:
a timid Dave, sometimes personable and other times less
so; and a tempestuous storm of a David Chang, culinary
icon, who could just as easily rip the skin from your face as
he could show you the technique behind his crispy, chewy
Korean-style rice cakes cooked in a pork ragu.

On this day, I tried to picture what had happened before I
had come to work, some meeting that had taken place before
I had come stumbling in with my sandpaper eyes. I imagined
Tosi, Chang, Salmon, a rat pack of outright and internalized
misogyny, gossiping about my dalliance with Johnny, aching to make some ill-timed joke at my expense. If the point
was to cut me down so that I would know my place in the
managerial hierarchy, then the trick had worked. Drew, with
whatever invisible help he had received before my arrival,
had scooped my spine from my lifeless body. He wasn't going
to fire me, he wanted me to know. He only wanted to hold
over me this pristine bit of knowledge, this perverse and
cruel window into my personal life.

Drew, finished with his flagellations, released me back
into the May sunshine. I dialed my father's number from my
BlackBerry. Should I quit? I wanted to know. On the other
end of the line, my class-action litigator father wanted to
know where else in New York I could work if not here. Hadn't
every other restaurant heard about me by now? Hadn't the
BLT bullies gotten to them, too?

My father was supposed to defend me, I thought, but I didn't feel particularly defended. My gut said: Run. Get out now. This man has shown you exactly who he is, and anyway, hasn't your time in restaurants proven that this business is cruel? Over and over again, I had been met with cruel circumstances, cruel people, cruel work hours. Why was I continuing to put myself through it? Chang was not in the room with us, but I surmised that he must have known, his specter in the dusty cellar with us like a terrifying ghost, screaming *chef-fucker, chef-fucker, chef-fucker.* And from there, it would only get worse.

Momofuku was, at the time, one of the city's most important restaurants. David Chang had been profiled in the March 2008 issue of *The New Yorker,* right around the time I had accepted the job. That 10,000-word Larissa MacFarquhar article, in all its brutal honesty, had somehow legitimized Chang to my own parents, who now saw him not just as a quotidian chef, but as a literary figure, of large enough import to appear in the only magazine that really mattered.

And so, despite my own reservations, and despite having been called a chef-fucker, I hung up with my dad and went back to work. There was nowhere else to go except back into that dark, dank cellar, where it was me and the wine and the man who had called me a chef-fucker.

*　　*　　*

Butter-Baked Peaches and Nectarines

Serves 10

5 firm medium yellow peaches (about 1 pound)
5 firm large nectarines (about 1¾ pounds)
½ packed cup (125 grams) dark brown sugar
½ cup (110 grams) demerara sugar
6 tablespoons (85 grams) chilled salted butter, cut into cubes
2 tablespoons dark rum
1 teaspoon almond extract
1 teaspoon vanilla extract
1 cup (237 grams) chilled heavy cream
2 teaspoons granulated sugar, preferably superfine

Preheat the oven to 350°F.

Remove any stickers and stems from the whole peaches and nectarines. Arrange the fruit in a rectangular or oval baking dish just big enough to fit them all in a single layer.

In a medium bowl, stir together the brown and demerara sugars. Scatter the sugars evenly over the fruit, then the cubed butter. In a liquid measuring cup, combine the rum, almond extract, and ½ teaspoon of the vanilla and pour over the fruit. Bake for 1 to 1½ hours, basting at least once during cooking, until the fruit is plumped and fork-tender; keep in mind that the peaches and nectarines may cook at different times; you can remove the cooked pieces and set them aside if they do. The pan sauce should be bubbling, and just syrupy enough to nap the back of a spoon.

Meanwhile, beat the cream in the bowl of a stand mixer fitted with a balloon whisk attachment (or with a hand mixer) on low speed until frothy. Increase to medium-high, add the granulated sugar and remaining ½ teaspoon vanilla, and beat for 3 to 4 minutes, just until soft peaks form. (You should have 2 cups.) Transfer to an airtight container and refrigerate until ready to use.

If you find that the sauce for the fruit is too thin, use a slotted spoon to transfer the peaches and nectarines to a platter. Give the sauce a good stir then return it to the oven to bake for another 15 to 20 minutes, until it is closer to a caramel.

Serve the peaches and nectarines warm, topped with several spoonfuls of the sauce and a plentiful scoop of whipped cream.

8 | TWENTY-EIGHT

The first thing that happened leading up to my 28th birthday, which fell on a thick and humid Friday in August, was that a Ssäm Bar manager allegedly overdosed and was found in the vestibule of his Alphabet City apartment building. For a day or two, he treaded the line between the living and the dead, cooped up in some New York City hospital room, in a coma—or so we heard through the restaurant grapevine. Then he woke up from the fever dream, blinked into the daylight, and was pushed back out onto the blistering city streets, where, pasty and thinned out from days without eating, he was sent home. He came into the restaurant a shell of himself, withered and pale, his gargantuan body bent over as he struggled to shuffle forward with the help of a cane. He didn't talk about it. Nobody did.

But the next day, Drew Salmon dropped by Ssäm Bar

to tell me that he planned to rewrite my entire schedule to accommodate for the manager's absence; he was being sent to California for three months to "study wine," everyone said, which was a glazed-over term used to avoid the discussion of what he'd really be doing there: rehab.

"I'm going to be staying with Abe Schoener," the manager told me before he left. Abe, winemaker for the Scholium Project in California, was an offbeat, 47-year-old former history professor who had moved to California from Annapolis in his 30s to pursue weird wine. When he was in New York, Abe liked to party, and party hard. He would show up with his black-rimmed glasses and a case of wine and sit down with whatever wine geeks happened to be around and order a bo ssäm—a slow-cooked pork shoulder with a crispy and sugar-caramelized top, served with kimchi, butter lettuce, and a dozen oysters—and slam back oxidative, full-bodied, high-octane wines until the restaurant closed.

This manager was not just a Schoener protégé; he was an obsessive. He loved Scholium Project wines with the same fanaticism that he loved the weird wines of, say, Slovenia. With Abe Schoener, anyway, a devotion to craft mattered. If you could sit in the dining room and shoot the shit about wine—if you could pretend that you cared about the process and the grapes and the sun and the aspect and the terroir while swirling a glass around at the end of a long night, saying things like *licking wet stone* and *barnyard* and *pencil shavings*—then you could hang with him as he opened powerhouse bottle

after powerhouse bottle, a veritable treasure trove of verti-
cals from opaque but so-called exceptional vintages that lived
somewhere in a mysterious bachelor pad cellar.

I had never found the Scholium Project wines interesting,
just like I had never found the thick, bombastic wines from
the label Sine Qua Non, which Robert Parker had elevated
to cultlike status, all that interesting. There were a million
ways to lay waste to a palate, after all. Why do it with a glass
of wine? But I often thought that the manager was more
enthralled with the giddy love language of winemaker than
he was with the actual language of wine, the expression of
where something came from or where it was going next. What
I had fallen in love with, like how a glass of Vosne-Romanée
could smell like a sunbaked raspberry patch in the middle of
July, did not seem to matter to the people who felt that wine
knowledge gave them a card-carrying pass in New York.

I don't know if the manager ever poured himself a glass
of Sylvain Cathiard's 2002 Vosne-Romanée aux Malcon-
sorts, a stunning, ruby-red elixir that summoned a berry
patch, a parcel of land with grapevines struggling to push
forth through the aches of nature. Wine was a time capsule,
I found, and when I was sad or nostalgic, I could drop the
tip of my nose into a glass and transport myself back in time.
There was Colin, always in True Religion jeans, sitting on a
case of wine in the cellar at BLT, holding up a bottle of Burgundy. "Say Chassagne-Montrachet one more time," and in
my fever dream, my glass of wine's conjuring, I would roll it

around in my mouth, my pronunciation clear and perfect, not like it had been in the years before, cluttered and incorrect, the fumbled French of an overeducated fool.

I pressed myself to remember the glasses of wine that I had loved before I had arrived at Momofuku, where slinging wine was more of a job and less of a passion, while the manager prepared himself to be shipped off to practice the fine art of winemaking with Abe, a discipline to kill whatever wants and desires had landed him in that predicament on that August evening—or this is what I had been told, at any rate. The manager would be going to California, and I had never worked a single season of harvest.

Sommeliers from all over New York were regularly invited on wine-related trips, but I had yet to see the world through my wine work. Instead, I was trapped working 15-hour days and slinging the wine that others had been drinking in caves in Burgundy and Champagne. I would also have loved the opportunity to stand in the vineyards of some far-flung wine destination, holding the grapes in my hands, measuring Brix, looking at the thickness of skin and learning the difference, in the field, between Cabernet and Pinot Noir. "I'll bet you can't tell me what it smells like in the Sistine Chapel," Robin Williams's character says to Matt Damon's Good Will Hunting in the titular 1997 film, and that's how I felt. I could describe the art, but I'd never actually seen it in person. What did I have to do to change my life, to escape the drudgery of the work I claimed to love?

I did not have the answer to this or any other questions, but I did know that my dissatisfaction was reaching a crescendo. The manager was leaving for California, and I would be left behind, selling more wine in his absence, working more hours in his absence, doing more, being more, just generally existing with more. I didn't know if a few months in Napa would chase away his demons or not, but it would definitely make life in New York more challenging for me.

"We're going to have to change your schedule," Drew told me, indicating that I'd be picking up the slack. That meant that my regular days off—Sundays and Mondays—would no longer be my regular days off while I covered for my manager.

That the manager's personal problems had become my own had me aggravated, but it felt like a small slight, like another condition of working in a restaurant. I had no real control over when or how I worked, and the same could be said for any of my colleagues, which was a fundamental frustration during the years that I worked the way that I worked. If it felt unfair and I expressed that perceived injustice, I would have just as swiftly been shown the door, because New York, like so many other states, was at-will, meaning my employer had no reason to keep me employed. It was my obligation to cover for my manager, just as it was my obligation to grin and bear it when my once-predictable schedule became categorically unpredictable and made it even more difficult to see my friends and family who worked more traditional jobs.

Still, none of this bothered me *all that much* until Drew

stopped by my office a second time, which was when the second thing leading up to my 28th birthday happened. Christina Turley, whom the general manager had hired not that long before, was coming to dinner at Ko on the night of my birthday. She had taken the night off.

"We're going to need you to wait on her and her family," Drew said, making it seem like it was a compliment, like I was the best person for the job, the cornerstone of Ko, a magical sommelier who could impress the empress of Napa. But I knew the truth. This was some kind of punishment, insidious torture for being a Momofuku outcast.

"It's my birthday," I said. It sounded ridiculous. I knew it, even as the words cascaded out. "I had requested the entire day."

In restaurants, if you want a day off, you have to request it weeks—or months—in advance, and I had done just that. We work hard for those tiny treasures, those finite moments carved from a restaurant's relentless hours of prep, which extend to both the kitchen and servers because a day in a restaurant does not begin when the guests arrive. It begins so many hours before, when food is prepped and when glassware is polished by hand. Even after the last check is closed out—even after the door is locked at midnight, at one in the morning, at four—there are the reams of paperwork spit out from the point-of-sale computer system, the closing of checks, the cleaning, the denouement, Act V, everything in its place before the curtain finally drops.

My plan had been to take the New Jersey Transit down the shore to visit my aunt and uncle, to jump into the green, frothy surf of Avon-by-the-Sea with my cousin, a rare pleasure skimmed off of my summer city work. With the manager gone, Drew said my trip was a no-go. No Sundays off, and, no, definitely not a Friday in August. I'd be spending my birthday in the throes of service, another reminder of the subtle inhumanities of restaurant work. Even when you tried—even when you planned months in advance to find a pocket of time to claim as your own—restaurants always found a way to purloin it, to take what was yours, that hard-earned time, that momentary flash of freedom. Sometimes, I felt that I had been fooled. Hadn't I gotten into restaurants because it had felt less confining to my free, creative spirit than working a proper 9 to 5? In the end, I was more beholden to the vicissitudes of managerial discretion than anyone in a salaried position.

A birthday is a small grievance. *It's just a day,* my mother would have said, but a day is much more than a day when a restaurant is your entire life, when you're meant to squeeze pleasure and enjoyment from the scraps left over from 15-hour workdays. And so, a birthday might feel like more than a birthday. It might feel like a respite from repetition, or from the ache of labor that you weren't even aware was baked into your bones. All I wanted was to crash headfirst into a cresting wave, the way my father had taught me to do at three, to ride it to its inevitable destination at the yellow lip of shoreline, and then to do it again and again until my body couldn't take it anymore. All I wanted was a little relief.

For months, the company had made it clear that they didn't much like me. Now, they were just making survival difficult for no reason. At dinner service, Turley walked in, her brown mane shining beneath the yellow lights of the dining room. The kitchen made tiny, beautiful plates and laughed giddily. Dave came—he was Dave this time—to entrance her family with his genial personality. They put on a very good performance. While the staff fawned, I snuck outside, smoked a cigarette, and cried about being two years away from 30. The number, 28, rolled around in my brain like a pinball. Thirty felt important. It felt like I was supposed to achieve a set of goals by the time I hit it, and I felt like I was nowhere near there. By 30, my parents had been homeowners, lawyers, parents. Most of my college friends were advancing steadily through their careers, now nine years in. But I was still in restaurants, still working weekends and negotiating for time off. Restaurants were a young person's game, but no one seemed to notice that I was aging out. Worse, no one wished me a happy birthday. Christina Tosi, who baked everyone in the company, from porter to busboy to server to manager, a birthday cake, somehow forgot about me.

But Momofuku systematically broke people down, and they did so on purpose, by making their staff feel unwanted. It was a Momofuku ritual to make a big show of presenting a many-tiered cake to every member of the Momofuku staff. A birthday tradition! A company-wide celebration! But when it came to the beverage director, me, that long-held tradition was conveniently ignored. I didn't complain, but I understood the inherent message. *It's an industry that doesn't love you back. They don't love you back.* It never really made sense, that a place that employed me would want so desperately to make me feel unwanted, would want so badly to disenfranchise members of the staff. But this was what Momofuku did as a means of control. They tore at us, moment by moment, until we were such tiny specimens that we could no longer remember why we didn't value ourselves any longer.

Christina Tosi. Andrew Salmon. David Chang. There were many offenders when it came to the restaurant's culture of pettiness, manipulation, and meanness. Momofuku pitted the front-of-the-house against the back-of-the-house, an already fraught relationship in restaurants. Chang loved to praise the talent of the kitchen while diminishing the usefulness of the servers, managers, and sommeliers. This only served to further divide a team that, in a perfect world, should work symbiotically. Instead, there was constant tension, and a constant issue of tips, which were split between the minimum wage–earning servers and the slightly higher-paid kitchen staff. It was easier to control people who were soft in the middle, the way I was. It was easier to create a culture where certain members of the team were insiders and certain members were outcasts, because those outcasts could be used to serve their purpose and then discarded when needed. We were tools in an arsenal, bodies to inhabit the spaces that needed filling for a restaurant group that kept growing and growing. The need for us existed. The love for us did not.

Once a person is tossed around enough—once a person believes that she has no real worth—that person will do pretty much anything you want her to do. I was an excellent test case for this theory. How many times had I come up against misogyny at this current position? Why hadn't I walked when Salmon accused me of being a chef-fucker? Why hadn't I gone directly through the doors into the midday sunshine when Chang had screamed *Who the fuck do you think you are?* at me in front of my staff, after I had purchased a bottle of Moscato for a Ko pairing? Why had I abided the unchecked schedule changes, the disrespect of having to serve another employee on my own birthday, and the final insult of the pastry chef flatly ignoring me, when everyone else in the entire company had received a cake?

I hadn't walked because I had nowhere to go. I hadn't walked because I was working for a notable chef at a notable restaurant, and I was convinced that it was better to be an unwanted member of a very cool party than to be a wanted member of a very uncool party—if I could even find an uncool party that would have me, and I couldn't even be sure of that. I hadn't walked because, somewhere in my mind, I was laboring under the delusion that if I did what

I always had done—which was apply hard work and discipline and strategy and intellect to my job on the floor as a sommelier—my employers would see the light and understand my value. How could they not? I was, I thought, a diamond in the rough, erudite enough to recognize Ira Glass on first glance, and chill enough to go out for a scorpion bowl after work.

What I was overestimating, of course, was how much value my employers put on the quality of my work. That wasn't what they cared about. Anyone could have stepped into my shoes and sold expensive bottles of wine to suckers on backless stools. They needed a warm body, and they needed a warm body who could be broken, who could be put to work like a mule. If you had asked me, before I found myself in restaurants, if I fit that description, I would have tipped my head back and laughed. Wasn't I too strong of a personality to come under the thumb of some abusive boss, some abusive industry? But anyone can get worn down, and time and a love for what I did had eroded my instincts. The only thing I knew how to do was survive, and I believed that my survival depended on staying in a job that fiercely wanted me to fail.

The fact that I didn't leave on my own—that I felt compelled to stay because the workplace was like a weird and unholy family—was another element of confusion. I felt strangely loyal to this place where I didn't truly feel welcome. I couldn't pull myself away from the drama, even as it harmed me. Stockholm Syndrome is probably a useful way to view how restaurant employees suffer through jobs of this nature. I was, after so much time in the broken system of restaurants, broken myself. I empathized with my abusers and, to some extent, I wanted them to like me. I also didn't know where else to seek employment. The only place I had ever really worked as an adult was in restaurants. Walking away meant seeking a whole new identity, and that felt just as scary and unpredictable as staying at a job that was tearing me apart.

It may feel petty to complain about being forced to work on your birthday, about being the sole member of the staff never to receive a cake. But I saw it then—as I see it now—as a tactic used to exclude me. I felt hopeless. That's how my employer wanted me to feel: hopeless. At Momofuku, toxicity was bred into the brand. There was an inhumanity to the work, but that was entirely the point: you were supposed to feel dispossessed of your humanness. For a long time, this worked. I believed that I was worthless. I believed David Chang when he told me that I was not good at my job. I believed him when he said that the cooks served a more useful purpose in the restaurant than the servers and sommeliers, and I believed him when he told me that I had no talent. I had been raised in privileged financial and racial circumstances, had attended an Ivy League university with no real debts, and, yet, even I had fallen victim to the narrative of abuse forced upon me by my employer. I had been convinced, after hearing this repeated over and over again, that it was true: that I was unworthy of better work; that I was unsuited for even the position that I held; and that I would never do better than I was currently doing.

I was the kind of person who fell into restaurants, too, because I was searching for something. I think that's fair to say. It was easy enough for me to stay because I had been looking for something that had been missing inside of me for a long time, and restaurants kept me looking. The ranks of restaurants are populated by tons of people like me: people who come from disrupted homes, people who don't know where else they belong in the world, people who have the kind of self-esteem that makes them believe that they deserve no better than a boss who tells them, as I once watched Chang say to a line cook, that he would happily scalp them and murder their family.

In some ways, I had reached a tipping point. The moments in restaurants had piled up. It wasn't just a cake. It was a cake and a man asking if I was a chef-fucker and a general manager who stole tequila and blamed it on me and a philandering boyfriend with his stupid copy of Neruda and all the little packets of coke in bathrooms and Bud Lights after work and hangovers and missed opportunities and all the days I said I'd stay home to write and didn't and all the friends I saw rising in the ranks at their real, grown-up jobs while I stumbled in from a cab ride with the sun blinking through the blinds. It was all of that, as I danced at the edge of 30, far too old now to be fucking around without purpose. It was time to get serious, but I hadn't gotten particularly serious about anything, and so my angst had turned into red-hot anger, roiling, boiling, unfortunately not unlike what Chang unleashed on whomever was close by when he happened to erupt. Only I wasn't erupting. I was disappearing.

Christina Turley brought the extremely potent (at somewhere around 15 percent alcohol-by-volume) Turley Zinfandel to dinner, of course, so there wasn't even any wine to sell to the Very Important Table. It was a waitress they needed, not a sommelier. They needed an erect body, not a person with a defined set of skills, certainly not a person who could drone on about the soil composition in Graves, on the left bank of the Garonne river, in Bordeaux. When does a fly know it has been caught in a spiderweb? When does late become too late?

My morale sapped, I dragged myself through more weeks of surly service. It's hard to love a job that doesn't love you back. I had known, somewhere, that restaurants did not love me, but some kind of proof was mounting, some kind of invisible tally. Was it Momofuku, or every restaurant? I couldn't really say. The hierarchy of cool—the indestructible structure of inclusion and exclusion—wasn't necessarily unique to Chang's restaurants, though I experienced it most acutely there. As August stretched into the first hot week of September, I felt like a beaten-down dog. Through the spring and summer, my parents had come into the restaurant to eat if they wanted to see me, because it was their only chance to catch a glimpse of their disappearing daughter.

"You work so much," my dad said. He was 54 and contemplating retiring from his law firm, where he had worked for 31 years. I couldn't relate to my father in this way. I couldn't imagine a world in which a person could work at one place for their entire working life. As a child, I had marveled at the things he kept in his desk: yellow legal pads, paper clips, and a tube of toothpaste, from the old days when he had to spend the night at the office. That had been a long time ago, though, before he had more pressing familial obligations. He had moved on, had established himself, and enjoyed a more reliable schedule. He must have forgotten the way it had been.

"Restaurant schedules," I had said by way of explanation. My father had mostly made time for other things, even through his most rigorous working years when he traveled for long cases in Oregon and California and Arizona. I couldn't remember a single time when his schedule had him home past dinner, or when he had to work holidays or birthdays. He had ended up in a career that had permitted him these civilities, these decencies. That toothpaste was probably from before I was even born.

He had started his job for Lowey, Dannenberg, and Knapp—it would later be called Lowey, Dannenberg, Bemporad, and Selinger—when he was still a law student at NYU. Back then, he had a job at the Museum of Natural History on the Upper West Side as an assistant for Margaret Mead. I now saw that my father, who had always had limitless other interests, may not have envisioned his life this way, either. Taking a job in the 1970s was supposed to be a steppingstone. Maybe it had just felt easier to stay.

Whatever the reason, he did stay, and that summer, in 2008, was his final summer as a practicing lawyer. In December, he would retire, intent, he told me, on doing other things to pass the time. He wanted to spend his time giving back. He wanted to teach, and he wanted to travel the world. He wanted to write a book about growing up on a converted poultry farm in Central New Jersey in the 1950s and '60s, the middle child in the maelstrom of a blended immigrant family, where a business of beach supplies and sundries flourished and where, for a time, my father got a little lost. He had never learned to ride a bike but had been excellent at calculating the precise moment you needed to jump headfirst into a wave to bodysurf it to shore. He could turn a perfect jackknife on my grandmother's diving board, depress the tongue down and then fly up in the air, touch his toes, and extend out straight again, an arrow heading straight for the water. To watch this athletic feat was to become a little breathless, because he made it look so incredibly easy.

Those were, of course, his extracurricular pursuits. He loved the water. He loved the mountains. He loved the quiet of a long run. But in work, he was consistent, and, in this way, we had lived different lives. His had been steady, a life of staying the course, of pushing through discomfort and even ennui. Meanwhile, I had left countless jobs behind and was now, at 28, the owner of a fragile career that boasted of very little: just a compendium of positions with no practical application in the real world, places that would not give me a stellar recommendation on paper, places where I had wasted my 20s, a decade that had stolen my youth while I had fallen madly in love, my passion unrequited.

"I don't know what to tell you, kid," he often said when I asked for advice. He was not an expert in restaurant life, though he would have done anything to end my torment. He could see it in me, I knew, the inability to grip onto anything, the lack of permanence.

If he had known that the cup of his life was draining, he would have been more instructive. That's what I like to believe now. I like to believe that he would have told me to assert my authority, to preserve my dignity, to walk out, to savor the last ripe moments of his life the way he savored every summer plum. Instead, we went on with our parallel lives, because time felt endless, the way that it does when you are 28 and your father is 54.

I needed someone to push me in one direction or the other and then, finally, Drew called me in September to meet in the corporate office on East 10th Street, and I figured: *Do I really have anything left to lose?*

September in New York was still warm, not at all like the Massachusetts of my youth. There was a kick in the air, but it was delicate, almost imperceptible. This was early September, still technically summer, hot by day, with cooled-off evenings. Harvest season. Somewhere, in some other region, farmers were getting ready to gather their clusters of grapes and turn them into wine. Some would pick them by hand, others by machine. Winemakers would roam the vineyards day after day, looking at the grapes and making judgments. Could the fruit stand another day of ripening? What did the forecast portend? One bad day of fall weather—a Caribbean hurricane winding its way up the Atlantic coast, for instance—could doom an entire vintage. But too little time on the vine had its consequences, too. Unripe Cabernet tasted like green bell peppers, like bitter tea.

In this start to the harvest season, I found myself on the culling table myself, although I didn't yet know it. I was headed for a visit with Drew Salmon, at his request. Official Momofuku firings took place in the main office, which was next to a lingerie store. Inside, it was far more sophisticated than my basement office at Ssäm, with its exposed pipes, imperfect wine storage, metal filing cabinets, and dusty computer. This was an actual office, with a few desks, a wash of modernist décor, and a handful of dedicated employees who called themselves Team Momo. They were mostly kids, some younger than me and a few around my age who were enthusiastic about the brand and who wanted to be a part of something. They were earnest, and they didn't know how to say no, and not knowing how to say no was probably the collective worst quality that we all possessed, as it facilitated the behavior of our superiors.

Drew asked me to sit down in front of his desk. He wore his standard outfit: khaki pants, button-down shirt, Converse All Stars, glasses. His affect was boyish, even though he must have been in his late 30s or early 40s. There was something about him that had always seemed a little desperate to me, like he was making up for something that he had never quite gotten his hands on in high school, some achievement of coolness that had never before been unlocked. What he didn't know was that the staff called him a narc behind his back. The more he tried to pal around with the people he worked with, the more he fomented deep feelings of distrust.

Not long before our current meeting, Drew had sidled up to me during service and made a comment about my waiter-boyfriend.

"A friend of mine saw you making out on the street corner outside of Ssäm," Drew had said.

I knew this to be categorically false. The waiter and I had been stealth in all our dealings. We had never once hailed a cab outside of work and we had certainly never been as forward as to display affection on a city street corner. I knew it because it had been a condition set not by me but by my staid suitor, who wanted to continue the illusion that we were nothing more than colleagues when we were in public. Drew was lying, and he was doing it to catch me in some kind of

HANNAH SELINGER

weird trap. He wanted me to confess to a private relationship, even though I had done nothing wrong. My employment agreement contained no fraternization clause. I had
made no promises that I hadn't kept.

"That didn't happen, I can assure you," I said.

Drew seemed surprised at my challenge. Perhaps he had
expected me to buckle at his accusation, but my alibi was airtight; no one had ever seen the waiter-boyfriend and me together
in a loving embrace. We were ghosts, our relationship a mirage.

I thought of this as I sat at Drew's desk. I thought of his
dishonesty, of how he had tried to trick me into confess-
ing something—for what purpose, I wasn't sure. From the
beginning, he had been uncomfortably interested in my sex
life, and his line of inquiry had led us here, to a place that I
presumed would not be pleasant.

"We're letting you go," he said, not parsing words. There
was no discussion of anything that I had done wrong. I had not
stolen anything, or fought with customers, or failed to get along
with my superiors. He did not mention the waiter-boyfriend,
knowing, of course, that the association also had not been a
violation of my contract, and knowing, too, that Christina
Tosi had been in a relationship with one of her subordinates.
It was industry standard, after all. I didn't have to do anything
wrong, of course, to lose my six-figure position at Momofuku.
That was part of the deep instability of my line of work, which
came with no severance pay, vacation time, or any specific or
long-lasting benefits. I had no safety net, and, in New York,

you don't have to do anything explicitly wrong to be fired; you just have to be the kind of person who doesn't fit in.

I nodded. For the entire duration of my time at Momofuku, I had assumed that a firing was imminent. When your position begins with the accusation of fucking chefs, there is no other way to perceive your worth to your company.

"They chose the weakest people, and they chose the people they categorically disliked," a friend recently said to me. She, too, is a restaurant veteran, and our experiences were similar. We were made to feel uncomfortable in our positions, like many people in places of employment. This is a common thread for outspoken women, for minorities, for people who just do not fit in. It's a constant reminder—particularly in New York, where you can be fired for no reason at all—that you need to be quiet and do your job. Toe the line without complaint. The people who succeed in environments like this are, largely, white men, because they "give no trouble." Those of us who are bullied, even on the most minimal level, are forced to swallow it. Reports to HR often go unaddressed. When we speak up, we lose our jobs. I lost my position at Momofuku for no disclosed reason. It's a known fact in restaurants—and, indeed, in plenty of hourly jobs around the United States—that speaking up against work-related abuse is a great way to guarantee that you will not have a position in the morning.

Drew asked for my BlackBerry, the bill for which was paid by the company. Without thinking, I handed it over, but the minute it left my hands, I was plagued with regret. I could feel it leaving my fingers as if in slow motion. What did he need it for, after all? He could easily lock me out of my email account. The rest of the information, after all, belonged totally and completely to me.

He looked at me and smirked. Then he plugged the phone into his computer for a few seconds and handed it back. I looked at the device, which was suddenly completely blank. I turned it off and then on again. Nothing. The address book was empty. My emails—all of them, years of them—were gone. Drew had erased all of the data, including my personal and professional contacts that had taken years for me to build. I had never bothered to memorize my parents' cell phone numbers. I didn't have them backed up.

"You took my personal information," I said to him.

"That all belongs to us."

"Does it?"

Drew looked at me without saying anything. It was time for me to go.

I walked outside, onto the sidewalk in the East Village, and I stared at my phone for a minute. It was late afternoon, and the sun was in between buildings when I looked west. There was a name for this—something like Stonehenge, Manhattanhenge, maybe—when the sun hits a certain spot, casting a glow between the buildings, but I couldn't remember it. On an ordinary afternoon, I might have found it beautiful, or calming, but on that afternoon, I found it blinding. That sun hit directly into my eyes, a piercing light that made it impossible to see. It hit me white-hot, inspiring not appreciation, but rage.

I looked at my phone again. It wasn't right, I thought. That hard work had been mine. The contacts had been mine. This had been stolen from me, and he had found the whole thing funny. He had taken so much more than my job, and he had looked at me, eyes smiling, and he had enjoyed the mastery and the sadism of it. He had enjoyed twisting the knife.

The door to the office was still unlocked. Drew and his office coworkers had not yet left for the day, though it was close to five. I opened the door and walked back in.

"Did you forget something?" Drew asked, looking up.

"I want my contacts back," I told him.

"I already told you," he said. "Those belong to us."

"They don't," I said. "I had those contacts before I worked here. You took my parents' phone numbers. You took professional contacts that took me years to build up."

"I'm not giving them back."

I sat down on a bench in the office. "I can wait," I said. "I can sit here until you give me back what belongs to me."

Drew looked increasingly uncomfortable. What were his options, really? To call the police for a trespasser? Technically *he* had stolen something from *me*.

"Give me your phone," he said. He plugged it back in, restoring everything, including every work email that had ever been on it. All of my Momofuku data reappeared. I walked out into the September Manhattanhenge sunshine, phone in hand. I had been released from something. I had been freed.

Drew gave me a gift that day, a late birthday gift, I guess. I didn't know that I had all of that in me the entire time, the ability to stand up for myself, the clarity to parse right from wrong again. The things that I should have said to him back when he called me a chef-fucker came roiling out. I wanted those contacts, the proof of my existence, the proof of the job, the things I had earned, my virtual Rolodex. It was mine, not his. Even if I ended up at another restaurant—and, yes, I would end up at another restaurant, though not for long—I wouldn't be the same person that I had been when I had walked into the Grog, or BLT, or Momofuku. Something was burning inside me now, born of self-preservation, or rage, or the knowledge that things could be better, that things shouldn't be like this. I had lit myself on fire, or all the years in restaurants had lit me on fire. I wasn't sure I knew the difference, but I knew that I had changed.

*   *   *

Carrot Birthday Cake with Cream Cheese Frosting

Serves 12 to 14 (makes a 9-inch three-layer cake)

CAKE

Unsalted butter, softened, for greasing the pans

2½ cups (300 grams) all-purpose flour, plus more for the pans

1½ teaspoons ground cinnamon

1 teaspoon ground ginger

¼ teaspoon freshly grated nutmeg

¼ teaspoon ground cloves

2 teaspoons baking powder

1 teaspoon baking soda

½ teaspoon kosher salt

3 packed cups (390 grams) trimmed, peeled, and grated carrots

½ packed cup (80 grams) golden raisins

1 cup (215 grams) canola oil

1½ packed cups (320 grams) dark brown sugar

½ cup (100 grams) granulated sugar

4 large eggs, at room temperature

1 teaspoon vanilla extract

FROSTING

16 ounces (454 grams) full-fat cream cheese, softened

½ cup (115 grams) unsalted butter, softened

1½ teaspoons vanilla extract

Pinch of kosher salt

4⅓ cups (535 grams) confectioners' sugar, sifted, or more as
needed

For the cake: Position racks in upper and lower thirds of the oven; preheat to 325°F.

Use butter to grease three 9-inch round cake pans with sides at least 2 inches high. Add enough flour to coat completely, tapping out any excess. Line with parchment paper rounds and grease them as well.

In a medium bowl, whisk together the flour, cinnamon, ginger, nutmeg, cloves, baking powder, baking soda, and salt. In a separate bowl, stir together the carrots and raisins.

In the bowl of a stand mixer fitted with a paddle attachment, combine the oil and brown and granulated sugars and beat on medium speed until smooth. (This can also be done by hand with a whisk.) On low speed, add the eggs one at a time, beating after each addition until incorporated. Working in batches, use a flexible spatula to gently scrape in the flour mixture, beating on low speed just until combined with no trace of dry ingredients. Add the vanilla extract. Stir in the carrot-raisin mixture by hand.

Divide the batter evenly among the cake pans, gently rapping them on the counter to release any air bubbles. Bake for 25 minutes, rotating halfway through, until lightly browned and a tester inserted into the centers comes out clean. Transfer the pans to a cooling rack to rest for 5 minutes. Run a round-edge knife around the inside edges of the pans, remove the cakes, and place on the rack to cool completely. (At this point, the cakes can be individually wrapped in plastic wrap and kept at room temperature for a day, or frozen for up to 1 month.)

For the frosting: In the bowl of a stand mixer fitted with a paddle attachment, combine the cream cheese, butter, vanilla extract, and salt, and beat on medium speed until smooth and well incorporated. Stop to scrape down the bowl. Add the confectioners' sugar about 1 cup at a time, beating on low speed until incorporated, then increase the speed to medium and beat until the frosting is smooth and creamy. If the frosting is not smooth or creamy enough, add more sugar, one tablespoon at a time, until desired consistency is reached.

When ready to assemble: Place a dab of the frosting on a cake plate, then set one cake layer on it right side up (to help anchor it). Use an offset spatula to frost from the center to the outer edges of the cake. Place a second cake layer on the frosting layer, top side down. Repeat the frosting method and then top with the final layer, this time top side up, and frost the top and sides.

Serve immediately at room temperature, or cover and keep at room temperature for up to 3 days, or cover and refrigerate. (The cake can also be frozen, uncovered, then wrapped in plastic wrap and kept in the freezer for up to 1 month.)

9 | DIAGNOSIS

Still, you have to get paid. That's the thing about restaurants, about self-realization, about all of the empowerment that comes with leaving a job and feeling momentarily enlightened. You still feel the squeeze. You still feel the drawing close of one month, the nearing of the start of the next one. My apartment in Astoria was either petite or grand, depending on which position you took. In the mid-2000s, for a single woman, it was a feat—practically royal, certainly bragworthy—to have one's own apartment. That apartment, though, had conditions. It had rent and electricity. I had to pay the bills.

I had enough in my personal coffer of savings—unusual for so many in the New York restaurant world—to float around for a few months without a job. And then I landed at another place, a newly opened Belgian bistro on East 29th Street, Resto, not too far from where I had spent all those years at BLT.

Rather than relitigate my old life, I took a different subway line in the morning, the 4, 5, 6. The former version of me had taken the R to 23rd Street, then walked the spine of Park Avenue, which burst to life with daffodils each spring, maintained by some invisible Parks Department force that was never seen or heard, but that must have existed, a New York mystery. Park Avenue had everything: a tidy Duane Reade and a far more expensive competing CVS; a mediocre slice joint and French Roast, a bistro that offered tripe 24 hours a day; a grocery store; and a bodega. At some point, I had walked into every one of these places, in search of one necessity or another. I didn't need to be reminded of the path I took during the time that I rose and crashed like Icarus. Utilizing a different train line meant complete avoidance of my old life, my old habits, the old streets I used to walk. New York City is like a graveyard of memories, some of which are better kept buried.

Managed by James Mallios, a slimy former attorney who spent more time trolling the halal carts than he did running the restaurant, Resto was small, with an ambitious menu. But the fryolator ran nonstop, producing Belgian-style fries made to order: potatoes peeled and cut, par-cooked, fried, salted in a giant silver mixing bowl—shaken vigorously to season all over—then sent out to the table while they were so scalding they took the skin off the roof of your mouth. A bowl with hot fries lived permanently on a metal table near the entrance to the kitchen, and it was the habit of every staff member to grab a fry or two when leaving. They were so hot that they truly did release the papery flesh, leaving the raw palate behind: pain in pursuit of pleasure. And yet, knowing what lay ahead, we all surged forward, digging our hands into the bowls, unable to stop ourselves, because the fries were delightful, because there was no way to stop, because we didn't know how to un-twin the powerful high of pain from the powerful high of satisfaction. If that wasn't restaurant work, what was?

I noticed it as he was getting back into the car at a stop on the New Jersey Turnpike, en route to my grandmother's seder. It was slight—just the way that he hesitated. It only took a second, but a flare ran through my brain, a lightning bolt. Stepping up to get into the car, my father was different, in a way that was both perceptible and imperceptible. We had stopped at a gas station, one of the ones that used to be a Roy Rogers. When I was younger, he and I had driven this route, through Brooklyn, across Staten Island, past the Fresh Kills dump and into New Jersey, stopping occasionally at a rest stop just like this one, where the gasoline was cheaper, and always, he always wanted me to know, full service. Roy Rogers was the fast-food joint where you could add as many pickles as you wanted to the burgers, courtesy of a condiment buffet—the Fixin's Bar—in the center of the restaurant, a joy for a child who loved the commotion, the ceremony, the dressing-up of food.

Had he been using the restroom, or buying himself a bottle of water? Whatever it was, when my father, a shade under 6 feet tall, slim, athletic, settling into middle age with gray stubble and wisps, now of brown hair that was creeping back, went to get into his car, he hesitated, leaned in and pulled himself up on the frame, like he needed assistance. It was as if his body couldn't do the work on its own, as if he needed the car—the steel frame of it—to pull him back inside. There was that bolt in me, sudden, eruptive. *He isn't OK,* the bolt said. *That isn't normal.* And then, without a word, we were back on the road.

I was training for my first marathon, I was thin, I was hungry, I ignored the impulse in the back of my brain that said that something was different. The food at my grandmother's seder was as normal as ever, the soup yellow and clear, the matzoh balls so hard they required a knife and fork. I dodged questions about work. "What's new with you?" my grandmother wanted to know. My limited success was always cause for concern at family events. My cousins were lawyers or therapists or skyrocketing toward success in the financial world. They were engaged and married, and I was single. They lived in houses they bought, and I rented an apartment.

When I was younger, my grandmother conducted the seders at her sprawling Central New Jersey home—a poultry farm converted into my family's beach sundry business—with puppets glued to popsicle sticks. There was

Moses, and Miriam, and the suffering slaves of Israel, and, for reasons that no one quite understood, a flock of sheep. The unluckiest among us always had to play the sheep in the recurring drama that was our family seder, wherein we read from an abbreviated Haggadah and enacted the plagues rained down from God unto Pharaoh while holding our characters. But the truth was, I had always felt like the sheep—a black one—the sole child of divorce, the unstable one, the one who was a little dark and unusual. Not much had changed between childhood, when certain aunts and cousins had tiptoed around me or ignored me or outwardly loathed me, and now. I was, still, the odd man out, adored by my father, forgiven by my grandmother, and looked at with a bit of derision by almost everyone else.

It's impossible to remember if I was feeling sorry for myself on the way home or if I was feeling steady, instead. We bypassed the city and drove straight to Westchester, to my father's house. I watched my father walk into the house. I swear I saw it again, whatever *it* was. A catch. Something he didn't want me to see. He went straight for the head of the kitchen table, and I went upstairs to change.

It was the night before Easter, a chilly April. My sister Julia was about to finish her sophomore year of high school; Emily, a decade my junior, was winding down her first year at Columbia. He called us into the kitchen, that large antique wooden table that was always covered with papers, then cleared for meals: placemats, cloth napkins, a nod to the importance of dining. You stopped the clock for dinner in this house. You talked about your day.

"Girls," he said, but we were no longer girls. I was 30, my sisters were adults, or nearly adults. Girls. We hadn't really been girls in years. Still, we were his girls. Someone had asked him if he had ever regretted not having any boys, but he said that he wouldn't have known what to do with them anyway. He made us fall in love with baseball the way he did, played Springsteen loud and sang along to the radio, taught me to drive a stick shift in a parking lot, and told me that I was terrible at tossing a ball. I couldn't play basketball the way he had, every Tuesday night, even into his 50s, until his hip started bothering him, but I could run, long and fast and hard, ignoring normal signals that normal people observed. When other people stopped running, I kept going, in heat and in cold, through pain and through mud and through rain, miles and miles logged. It didn't bother me. I was ferocious, an unlikely athlete. His girl.

"I want to talk to you about something," he said. He had taken on his lawyerly tone. At the law firm, my father had been the person tasked with letting employees go. It wasn't because he was mean or authoritative; it was because he did what he said he was going to do, and it was because he executed tasks with compassion. He was a grown-up. Here in the kitchen, I could feel him slipping into his grown-up role, changing the way he changed in the mornings when he put on his Zegna shirts and Armani suits, clean-shaven, pressed.

It had started in his leg, he said, back in January.

"I noticed," I said. "When you were getting into the car."

"You never miss anything," he said. "I can count on you for that."

During those Tuesday night basketball games, he had noticed some trouble with his lateral movement.

"I thought I was just getting older," he confessed. "Except it started getting worse." He went to a series of doctors, none of whom had any answers. Eventually, after a few months, he was referred to a neurologist. "It's basically something called motor neuron disease, or PLS," he said. "They only just gave me a diagnosis a few weeks ago, and we wanted to wait until we were all together to tell you."

I had heard that term before. *Motor neuron disease.* I rolled it around in my head. I couldn't remember why it sounded so familiar. My father answered some questions. What would happen next?, we wanted to know. He might begin to walk with a cane; the truth was, he had already been fighting a bit of a leg drop. And after that? Well, the neurons in his body, which communicated signals to his muscles, might stop communicating. And it was possible that the disease could progress, stopping other essential systems from properly functioning.

He reported this quietly, without emotion. I could tell from his ice-blue eyes that there was something he wasn't saying. When I had been younger, I would ask plenty of questions that my father didn't want to answer. *How much money do you*

make? None of your business. For all of his honesty, and for all
of my limitless curiosity, there was a line with my father, a
boundary, his secrecy, the world that belonged only to him.
I had found myself up against that boundary again, there in
the April kitchen, new growth pushing through the ground
outside, crocuses, daffodils. It wasn't only T. S. Eliot who
associated this month with cruelty, the nakedness of spring's
rebirth. A few months before my 14th birthday, during a cold
spring, I had walked home from school—those purple flowers just making their way through frozen earth—to learn
that my musical icon, Kurt Cobain, had shot himself at his
home in Seattle. He was 27 years old, now a young man by
comparison. It was strange to realize that your idols could be
immortalized in youth, to know that you could catch up to
them, surpass them, out-age them.

It was, of course, another cruel April. My father sent us
to bed, but instead, I went upstairs, to the computer, and
input "motor neuron disease" into the search engine and
found photos of one of my father's favorite baseball legends,
Henry Louis Gehrig, who played 17 seasons with the New
York Yankees as a first baseman until he retired at age 36.
He had been diagnosed with a disease that was then mostly
unknown, amyotrophic lateral sclerosis, a "'creeping' paral-
ysis," as he wrote to his wife, Eleanor, in 1939. That disease,
I learned, was first called Lou Gehrig's disease and would
later be abbreviated to ALS. The muscles lose their ability
to receive transmissions from neurons. The body dies, from

the extremities inward. It takes years, but not many of them. The foot drops first. Then the hands curl. Eventually, the body cannot perform normal functions, like peristalsis, or breathing. Eventually, it's fatal.

So many years ago, when those planes had flown into buildings, I had experienced a loss of time, the broad expansion of days and weeks that lived larger in my memory. How long had we sat on the floor of our dorm room, watching the news? It felt like a month. It was probably only a few hours. From the moment those three letters appeared on the screen of my computer, time compressed in me again, a recalculation of my life. A hitch in the hip—*something isn't right*—had mutated into something else, something insidious. The clock had stopped. How long had I been sitting at that computer, anyway?

In the morning, Easter morning (not a holiday in our agnostic-Jewish household), the elephant of my father's disease had left the room. My father wore Converse sneakers and jeans and a T-shirt. He was young. He looked young, young enough to resume his Tuesday night basketball regime. He was only 55. There was still time. Wasn't there still time?

"I'll drive you in," he said. He had always been that kind of father, quick to give over his time, fine with sitting in an airport if it meant hearing me play "Under the Sea" in a 4th grade violin recital, fine with sitting in an airport longer if it meant not missing me sing 10 notes in *It Takes a Wizard,* my 5th grade role of a lifetime as Guard Number 2; he had gotten stuck in a snowstorm somewhere between La Guardia and Logan. When the alternator of my Volkswagen went out three days before Christmas as I was on the Hutch driving friends to Massachusetts for the holiday, he picked us all up, drove us back to his house, fed us, and lent me the keys to his Audi for the weekend. He had been an active, participating dad, a *dad* in the realest sense of the word, the kind of parent that I could hope to be in an outline of a vague future but that, let's face it, so many people really never live up to.

"OK," I said, I'd let him drive me, I'd accept his kindness, I'd continue to be daughtered by him until, at some point, that reality would be impossible. That day wouldn't be far off. He could extend one final bit of protection to me—a ride into the city, a piece of parenting—and so he did.

In the car—the last car, I now realize, that my father would ever drive, just a stupid Passat station wagon when he could have driven a fun little car, even a Toyota Tercel stick shift like in the old days, although there would never be any old days again—he seemed like himself. No hesitation. Just a 55-year-old guy with a little gray stubble, an ex-runner, still into sports. He'd run if he could, and you could tell, just by looking, that he had always been fit. Sure, he liked frozen custard from the Jersey Shore, but he also sprinkled intolerable wheat germ on his cantaloupe in the mornings; he was that kind of guy.

"What do you want to ask me?" he said.

But I didn't want to ask anything. I didn't want to know what the lifespan of someone with ALS was, because I already knew: two to five years, unless you were Stephen Fucking Hawking, and my father was probably not Stephen Fucking Hawking. I already knew, without having to ask, that my father would decline extreme measures to save his life. No life on a respirator. Maybe no feeding tube. I couldn't imagine him in a motorized wheelchair, his voice replaced by a computer. But ALS had a pattern, and that pattern was undeniable.

"I don't want to ask anything," I said.

"You don't have questions?"

A chasm of silence opened. I watched the landscape change from tony Westchester, forsythia pushing yellow blooms, into city smog, Yonkers into the Bronx into Manhattan. Concrete barriers, affordable housing, a sea of windows with tiny balconies, people making the best of it with their houseplants, views of the East River, which was also gray. I wondered what it was like to grow up with that view, to look out on the water from a tall building and to see the slick, slippery waterways of New York. I had once read that the currents in the East River could run as fast as five knots per hour, twice as fast as the current on the opposite side, in the Hudson.

The drive into the city, in my youth, had felt silver and promising, trips to the United Nations and the Rockefeller Center tree and lunch at Flower Drum on Second Avenue. Now it just felt gray. New York felt gray, the prospect of going back to restaurants felt gray, the grim prospect of what I was doing—*what the hell was I doing?*—felt gray. For years, I had begged off seeing friends and family in favor of some specter of career development, and now I was paying the price. You don't get the time back. For 30 minutes, from Larchmont straight to work in Gramercy on the skeleton-framed highway, lonely, a ghost town on Easter morning, my father and I sat in silence, contemplating life and death, or missed opportunities, or all the things that we still had time to say but weren't yet ready to.

At Resto, the dining room felt a little electric, like the way a field feels in summer just before a thunderstorm. I walked in puffy and beaten down, soft from the inside out, ready to bare my soul to the first person who asked—but no one did. I saw servers and bartenders tucked in, readying the restaurant for service, cutting citrus into perfect segments, folding napkins, polishing glassware. In the office downstairs—a tiny, windowless basement office, like nearly all restaurant offices—I found James Mallios, the pallid general manager, sitting at the computer, waiting for me. I had barely entered the door when he started talking.

"Hi. Good morning. I'll stay, say, for an hour and then you can take the double," he said. He was leaving to celebrate Easter.

"I have to talk to you about something," I said, shutting the door behind me.

"OK," James said. He was tapping his foot, the urgent energy of a restaurant person who wanted to get out *now,* whose shift had expired *like five minutes ago,* even though it was ten in the morning.

"Last night, I found out that my father has ALS. I don't know if you know what that is."

A blank stare.

"It's basically. It's. His brain stops telling his muscles what to do?"

A blank stare.

"First his outer extremities will stop working? And then he will stop being able to speak? Eventually—like, in a few years—he will no longer be able to breathe, because his brain will stop telling his respiratory system to do that kind of stuff, too?"

Another blank stare. At this point, I was, probably, to him, just another untidy, hysterical woman, unable to keep my shit together.

"Well, I'm sorry about all that," he said, avoiding eye contact. "Take some time if you need it." With that, he scurried from the room like a New York subway rat, messenger bag bumping him in the rear.

I worked my way to the wine room, where I pulled out a case. Since the night before, I hadn't had a chance to do anything. I had called no one. I had consoled myself with the kindness of no one. James had been the first person I had divulged my upcoming loss to; not even my mother knew about my father, and she had been married to him for a decade. In the cellar, I called friends who knew my dad and friends who knew me. I called family. I screamed and sobbed until a server came down to tell me that the restaurant was busy, and that there was no one in charge. James had left the restaurant unmanned, with me in the cellar, figuring out how to survive.

I would have stayed. I would have clenched my teeth and stayed because I wanted to prove that I could endure pain. I was, after all, in the throes of training for my first marathon, up in the mornings and forcing myself to do a thing I had always thought I hated, training myself to love the repetition of the road, one foot in front of the other, over and over and over again. On those long and lonely mornings, where I learned to see the shifting shapes and contours of the city—here was a tree in March, gray sticks, now April, green with the unfurling promise of a bud—I lost time in the rhythm of the road.

The art of distance running has little to do with natural talent and everything to do with how long you can sink into the pain. It's true that I had become comfortable, long before I had made it to the road, with the familiar pathways of pain, how they had burrowed inside of my body, twinned to me. Somewhere in the middle of a run, the so-called runner's high: you feel like you can run forever. The art of running is learning to ignore this fundamental part of the brain's messaging system, to excavate pain, to make it palatable. I had made running palatable, I had made restaurants palatable, or, otherwise, my brain had mixed up love and pain or love and hurt or love and death, the conflicted and confusing emotions that all live on the side of a cliff together.

And also, I wanted to stay in love with restaurants. The place where restaurants and love lived simultaneously was, to me, still exciting, and still nostalgic, and I didn't want to lose it. My father, who had lived in New York while I grew up with my mom in Massachusetts, had helped me fall in love with food, and leaving restaurants still felt like some kind of move away from a thing that he loved. For my 20th birthday, he took me to Gramercy Tavern, and when the captain came along with dessert, my father ordered a selection of cheeses from a cart, golden honey swirled onto a plate with intention, truffles produced whimsically from a glass jar, delicate dried fruits, a whole artistry to cheese—foods I believed belonged in the deli section of a grocery store, and a thing I had never seen. I didn't understand how a person could eat cheese at the end of a meal.

A few days after that Easter brunch, James called me down into the dungeon of the office. I could sense a predictable routine. Close the doors. No witnesses. Just me and the boss, together again.

"I'm going to have to let you go," he said.

It was my turn to stare blankly. I looked at the wall. At the dusty computer screen, where James sat every day. Didn't the dust bother him? No one seemed to care about how dirty it was down there. I would have cleaned it. I would have done a lot of things.

"It just isn't working out."

"Sure," I said. "I understand."

"We're going in a different direction."

Restaurant managers are cagey when they fire you. Men hate to look women in the eye, preferring to disseminate pain quickly, sharply: you take the blow while they slither away. It's an abstract fear of emotion that plagues the managers who will fire you, annihilate your career in minutes as they turn on their heel. You aren't right for the job. They're going in a different direction. This isn't working out. Why? It's not them, it's you. There's no real reason that they can give you, besides an irritation. It's the way you assert yourself, or the sound of your voice, or how you stood up for yourself. Or it's the fact that your father is dying and they're afraid that your tenderness is a burden that the toughness of a restaurant can't handle. All the softness of a woman—all the baked-in emotion of a woman who is bound to break in and down in the aftermath of tragedy—can't possibly be a fit for a restaurant. Send her away. Send her back out into the gaping, needy world.

I have no proof that I was fired for telling my employer that my father was diagnosed with a terminal illness, only the vague suspicion that my humanity triggered a response of something less humane, that they saw in me a threat: That

I would leave; that I would need to redirect my attention; that I would be moody or unstable; that I would have to go to a hospital or a house now and then; that I would have priorities that were not the restaurant. I should have voiced these suspicions, but I said nothing, because nothing was easier, or more comfortable, or because I had been convinced that nothing would change anyway, that nothing could ever change.

It was, for me, an indignity. Later, I would think of my father's colleagues at the law firm. Those men and women would come calling immediately. They would ask what they could do to help. But I had no colleagues of note. I had coworkers who had stared through me, who called me into a cellar office to let me know they were "going in a different direction." I wanted to scream. I wanted to thank them for exposing the muscle, the rotting meat of the industry, its rotting corpse of humanity. When my friend Artie died, I had to beg to take the day off for his funeral. I still don't know why my brilliant friend killed himself at 28, but I did know, even then, that a night with my college friends, remembering his rapacious wit, was more important than serving wine to people from New Jersey.

I did not want to leave restaurants. But restaurants—the culture of restaurants—then, or now, or forever, believed in a limit to what a human being could feel or express or do. In the deep hollow of me, I knew that it was impossible to both be in restaurants and be a caretaker, to be in restaurants and live a life that felt normal. No one had made a provision for that, and I wasn't equipped to make a provision for it myself, either. Was it my failure, or the failure of an industry that had been erected around the premise that workers were disposable, that signs of weakness included emotion, hunger, pain, and any true corporeal need? I didn't know then, but I do now.

A few years after I left Resto, in winter, my father, stepmother, and I went to dinner at Blue Hill at Stone Barns, in Pocantico Hills, my father's favorite restaurant. By then, I knew just as much about food and wine as my father once had. I could tell him everything about the rainfall in his storied 1982 first-growth Bordeaux collection. I could talk to him about Époisses. We sat down in the dining room of a place that my father had loved, and his hands shook when holding a fork. The courses came out slowly. He was in a wheelchair by then, no longer ambulatory, his motorized apparatus calling attention to us wherever he went. When a charred rutabaga came out, a bespoke plating meant to represent the cold weather bounty, my father rolled his eyes. "I hate rutabaga," he said, under his breath, once the servers had gone, and I knew that the magic of this kind of place had expired—not just for him, but for all of us. What could we find here that we could not find just as easily at home with one another?

By then, the mystery of restaurants was long gone. I knew the secrets of the cheese boards, how the servers would slice the trimmings from them after service each night, how the custom and courtesy that goes on out in the open, before guests, is less likely to be observed in the back, when no one is watching. The first time I had been to Stone Barns, also with my father, it was like a light switch had been turned on. We had arrived in time for summer's last gasp: hearts of Brandywine tomatoes on spikes attached to a wooden board; Thumbelina carrots; fairy-tale eggplant dusted with sesame seeds; a single egg presented in the cradle of a basket as a midcourse delight. Each unraveling dish had been a revelation, a window into the farm and its mystical world, food cared for, a world where anything was possible.

Years later, black-charred rutabaga in front of us, Stone Barns didn't feel as appealing. My father pushed his plate away. Actually, it had all been a lie anyway. That butter? According to allegations from former staff members, it wasn't local at all. Like everyone else, I saw what I wanted to see, until it was impossible to see anything besides what was right at my own table.

"We don't have to come back here, you know," I told my father that night. His suit looked uncomfortable. His hands had curled up—a common problem with ALS patients—and he held his silverware in balled fists. He had long since given up trying to cut his own meat. He was waiting for us to grant him permission, for me to grant him permission. It wasn't just Stone Barns that he had lost interest in, but food and restaurants in general. He wanted cold custard, frozen, from the New Jersey Shore, the kind he had as a boy. He didn't want to eat vegetables or wear sunscreen.

He sort of nodded, a concession to his old life, now fading, a life of restaurants. He was leaving them, I was leaving them, we were leaving them together. If the restaurant knew that it was catering to the ambivalent—to the silently unhappy—it gave no sign of it. Designed to act as if nothing was ever wrong, even if the infrastructure was rotting from within, the show went on, forceful and mighty, course after course, a processional, right up until the bitter end.

My moment in restaurants, as it happened, had expired. It had expired before that dinner at Stone Barns, before the blackened rutabaga, that root-vegetable harbinger of rot and decrepitude. I would work in restaurants again, for a slip of a summer, but my time at Resto was my final stab, my last substantive full-time restaurant job. I hadn't known, when I walked out the door for the final time, that I was looking back on an entire body of work, an arc of circumstance and accident, choices that belonged both to me and to other people. If I had fallen into restaurants, if I had stayed of my own volition or from inertia, the last step out the door onto 29th Street was a step that felt different. You don't always know that something is ending when it is, in fact, ending.

I did not wake up one morning knowing that I wanted to leave my job, but my father's condition stood as a good excuse—as good an excuse as any—to walk away from something that had tied me up for a decade of my life, a con-strictor, tightening, suffocating. Restaurant folk like to talk about how free we are from the confines of traditional society. We can go grocery shopping in the middle of a Tuesday after-noon. We have so much time to dedicate to our craft, we say. The work, it's only meant to fuel the creative energy, to propel us forward while we write our novels, our screenplays, while we become actors and citizens of the arts. But I couldn't remember the last time that I had written anything of substance, besides a carefully worded email or a saccharine love letter to one former boyfriend or another. My writing had taken a backseat to long nights at the restaurants, long nights at bars. Wine, I had tried to convince myself, was as useful a creative impulse as any, a worthwhile firing exercise in intellectual capacity.

But it wasn't true.

Learning about wine was stimulating, but it didn't set me on fire. Only writing could do that. When I was younger, I had dreamed up a start-up literary magazine with a friend. We had made a pact; if we still failed to live our bookish American dreams by 29 and 30, we would quit our jobs and open a bookstore, like the Strand, but better.

But my friend had spent years working for George Soros's Open Society Institute before accepting a high-profile posi-tion as the assistant director of photography (and then, later, the director of photography) at *The New Yorker*. She was a month from turning 30 and I was four months from turn-ing 29, and there was no bookstore. The informal contract, written on ruled notebook paper in Sharpie, still lived in a hanging file in my Ikea cabinet in my apartment, but we had made no provision for what would happen if one person fulfilled her dreams and the other did not.

The true freedom, I realized, had come in the loose unraveling that had started in my final years in restaurants. If the action of standing up to Drew Salmon had opened a door for me, my transformation from *restaurant person* to *real-world person* became complete the moment I found myself out on the street for that final time, blinking in the daylight, a woman with no evening commitments. I mostly felt cheated, like time had been stolen, like the things that I loved were eroding, like I didn't have a place to be at any set time. But the truth was, I had never really been free to do the things that I had set out to do when I had signed on to work at restaurants. I had never written any Great American Novel. All the people who had seen some fiery creative capability in me had long since moved on with their lives.

Even though I suddenly had plenty of time to do the work that I had been avoiding for a decade, I spent a lot of time doing very little besides shuttling between my father's house in Westchester and my apartment in Astoria, and hitting the New York Sports Club on 30th Avenue, and going to the matinee in Long Island City with my friend, who reminded me that it was OK to change out of my sweatpants every once in a while.

"I'm going to stage an intervention," she told me one day. "You have to stop wearing sweatpants as if they are real pants."

But outside of restaurants, I began to feel driven by purpose. When my father's hands curled into fists, I opened his mail and input his bills into Quicken. When he stopped being able to swallow, I made him banana milkshakes. When he wanted to write a book about his New Jersey childhood, I typed the words out on his computer. I sent his emails and put on his favorite CDs and adjusted his iPad so he could watch the Yankees games. I helped with the Hoyer lift so that he could get in and out of bed once he could no longer walk.

I also enrolled in night classes at the French Culinary Institute while I cared for my dad during the day. I had started culinary school to pass the time, and to prove something to myself and to the chefs I had worked for, so in the evenings I went to SoHo to practice brunoise and to learn my mother sauces. I learned how to slice an onion, how to make pastry cream, how to turn blocks of butter and piles of flour into flaky pâte feuilletée. In tilting steam kettles, I made veal stock for 10, for 20, for 30, for 100, mixing mirepoix with roasted bones, stirring and holding my face over the scalding liquid for long enough to forget that David Chang had once told me that I lacked the skill to do exactly this, to make excellent food, because I was just some front-of-the-house hack. Later, I would come back and make custard for my father, never curdling the eggs, because I took my time, because

I was patient, because I believed in the process. Before he died, the sour cherries were just coming into season, the way they do in those last, ripe days of June, and I folded them into custard, but my father was done eating by then anyway, had given up even on his final joys: something soft and sweet in the mouth. He would not make it to see the summer's plums, his favorite.

By the time my father was entering hospice care at home, I was staging in the school's tiny restaurant, making dishes that he would have loved, if he still cared about food, tiny gnocchi that I spent hours preparing in the garde-manger station before picking them up hot for service; they got fried to order, a handful to a plate, crisp on the bottom in beurre noisette, brown butter, and served with two sprigs of fried sage that was part of the mise-en-place that I cooked before the evening began. My father never tasted those gnocchi, and I never made them again after he died, not once, not even as a comfort to myself.

On the morning that he died, I took off my sneakers and lay on the bed next to him. I didn't have to be at work because I didn't have another job. A few weeks later, a few months later, I would sit down at the computer again. I would start to write, first about cooking—about tearing the heads off of live lobsters and about grief—and then about my father. I would write about love and about not knowing who I was and I would write all of this for no one in particular. I would write about peanut butter and jelly sandwiches and about how you could eat them with Lambrusco. My muscles would remember how to write. I would feel alive with it, with the pulse of writing, with how much came out if I pushed just a little.

"What did you think Hannah would be when she grew up?" a family member asked my mother, a decade later.

"A writer," she said, with confidence. How had she known all along when I had been unsure? I had been muddling through restaurants, reluctant to rely on writing talent, convinced that artists cannot survive, that the only pathway to art lay in toughing through restaurants. In some ways, I was reborn through this tragedy, pink and new in the world, without the shell of restaurant work to protect me. I was reborn, made new, like a baby lamb starting in the newest season, just waiting to spring to life.

*   *   *

Pan-Fried Gnocchi with Brown Butter and Sage
Serves 4 to 6

2½ pounds russet potatoes (about 4 large), scrubbed well
¾ cup (90 grams) all-purpose flour, plus more as needed
2 teaspoons kosher salt, plus more as needed
1 large egg, lightly beaten
½ cup (115 grams) unsalted butter
2 tablespoons olive oil

20 fresh sage leaves
4 garlic cloves, thinly sliced
Freshly ground black pepper
2 teaspoons fresh lemon juice
¼ cup (25 grams) grated Parmigiano-Reggiano cheese,
    for serving

Preheat the oven to 425°F. Set a small ovenproof rack over a rimmed quarter baking sheet. Place a long piece of parchment paper on your work surface, and line the rimmed baking sheet with parchment.

Use a fork to prick the potatoes all over and set them directly on the rack on the baking sheet. Roast for 70 minutes, or until they can be easily squeezed and their skins are crisped. Transfer to a cutting board, immediately cut the potatoes in half lengthwise, and scoop out the flesh. Working in batches, press the hot potatoes through a ricer onto a clean work surface. Let cool.

In a bowl, whisk together the flour and salt. Pour the beaten egg and the flour-salt mixture over the riced potatoes and use your fingers to gather and gently work the mixture for about 2 minutes, until just incorporated, forming a smooth dough. Transfer to a pastry bag fitted with a ½-inch round tip (or use a resealable zip-top bag with a bottom corner cut off on the diagonal).

Dust the parchment with flour. Squeeze out the dough and then roll it into 24-inch-long ropes that are approximately

½ inch thick. Cut them crosswise into ½-inch pieces and lightly dust with a little more flour (to avoid sticking), keeping them on the parchment as you work.

Heat a large pot of water over medium heat until barely boiling. Add a good pinch or two of salt; once it has dissolved, reduce the heat to medium-low. Working in batches and without crowding the pot, add the gnocchi and cook for 3 to 4 minutes, until they float to the surface and have roughly doubled in size. Use a slotted spoon to transfer them to your baking sheet.

Melt 2 tablespoons of the butter in a large nonstick skillet over medium-high heat. Once it's foamy, add about one-third of the gnocchi, tossing to keep them in a single layer. Cook for about 5 minutes, until golden and crisped, turning them as needed. Transfer to a plate. Repeat two times with more butter and the remaining gnocchi; adjust the heat as needed to avoid scorching, and wipe out the pan between batches.

Melt the remaining butter and the oil in the same skillet over medium heat. Once it has started to brown and develops a slightly nutty aroma, add the sage leaves, shaking the pan to coat them evenly. After 2 minutes, stir in the garlic and cook for another minute, until fragrant. Return all the sautéed gnocchi to the pan, tossing to coat. Taste, and season with salt and/or pepper.

Remove from the heat and stir in the lemon juice. Divide the gnocchi among individual wide, shallow bowls and serve with the Parm.

10 | THE HAMPTONS

ust when I thought I was out..." my father used to say, when anyone mentioned *The Godfather Part III*, everyone's least favorite Godfather movie. It's an iconic line from a less-than-iconic film, but I think of it often in the framework of my life in restaurants. I have been in and out and back many times, though it has been the pulse of restaurants—and not a family associated with the mob—that had pulled me, like a riptide, into the outer reaches.

I have allowed myself to be carried by the rip of restaurants. Like any rip, it's impossible to know how far you've drifted until you're out. What might seem like an easy swim at Ditch, Montauk's famed surfing beach, can turn on you. Look back too late and you're a mile from shore, even if you're a cautious and expeditious swimmer, which I am.

*   *   *

In 2013, two years after my father died, I took a summer job in the Hamptons, working the floor five nights a week as a sommelier at Nick & Toni's, the market-driven Italian restaurant known best among the Hamptons elite for how its VIP book read like the program at an awards ceremony. In coming back to restaurants, I had been aiming, first, to return to the ocean, to baptize myself in the Atlantic and to remind myself of the things my father loved: his clean jack-knife into any body of water on a clear summer day, his fear-less willingness to ride a wave to the shoreline. That wound in me was so fresh that I still needed to throw myself into the blue water, cold and deep, to recover from the blinks. *One for yes, two for no.*

Every July, I still woke with beads of sweat forming across my brow, my heart beating furiously in my chest. I was still plagued with a recurring dream, the one where my dad had never been dead. He had died on July 9, 2011, seven days after entering hospice care at home, all mortal worries soft-ened by the humane care of morphine.

In the final days of my father's life, we wrapped up the duties of the living. We canceled his credit cards and his cell phone. We listened to a stack of CDs that he had selected: Joni Mitchell, one last time, he decided, even though he could no longer sing along. His favorite Springsteen. He had been a true believer in the power of New Jersey; I knew of no other fan who could say that they had seen the Boss in concert more than 300 times. But the things that had brought my father the most joy had already died. He could not eat frozen custard; for months he had been surviving from a feeding tube connected directly to his stomach. He could not mimic Max Weinberg's percussion on "Born to Run." He couldn't sing, or play basketball, or go for a walk with the dog. He was tired.

For a while, in that hot July week that turned out to be the final week of my father's life, I read emails from friends and family to him, but then, as the 4th of July slipped into the 5th, 6th, 7th, I could see that he no longer wanted to hear messages from the present, soon to be the past. He could not shake his head, but he could blink: once for yes, twice for no. Did he want me to read the one from Marilyn, his sister-in-law, peeling herself back, telling him the way she loved him? Two blinks. I read it to myself and deleted it. So much about the end of life is also about the final choice to be free to do exactly what you want with it.

In my recurring dream, it was all a mistake, the part where I stood in the Westchester kitchen at seven in the morning on a broiling Saturday in July, cutting lobster into neat cubes and mixing it with mayonnaise, celery, chives, busying my hands with the duties of service while my father, upstairs, was busying himself with the duties of dying. In the dream, my father is back; he is alive. I ask him where he has been during these gap years, the years where we have carried on, living in the absence, the incomplete life without him.

"It was all just a joke," he says. He says this every time, or some variation of this.

"It's a terrible joke," I always say. I am angry that anyone could find this funny, and also relieved that he was never really dead. It could be one year since his death or a thousand. Time is meaningless in this dream, though I have some vague concept of it, a half-conscious understanding that I will wake up to the same bleak reality: dead dad, incomplete lobster salad, unfinished plans. Why he visits me in this way—a bitter joke, I guess, emblematic of his always slightly sour sense of humor—eludes me, though I like to think of it as a waiting room for ghosts. My mind is open just a crack in this space between midnight and dawn, with a gap wide enough for benign spirits to slide in.

In the space between when he died and where I still lived, I finished culinary school, worked the entremetier station, where I broke down entire lobsters. They were still alive. I cracked at their shells with the back of my knife, ripped their heads off with my bare hands, thought about life and death and disease and the brain and how quickly a thing could end. But first, I had to return. I walked in on that brutal day back to find my classmates waiting for me with a card of sympathy. Only Angie Mar, who would go on to run flashy but boring New York restaurants, declined to sign it. She wasn't a superlative cook, but she was ruthless, and I knew, standing in that locker room on my first day back to change into my whites, that she would find success as a chef, because she had exactly what it required: a lack of empathy, the ability to muscle through, a grisly disposition. I saw that mean visage. I saw through her—into her—and I knew, for a moment, what it would take to be like her, to be the kind of chef who rose to the top but in the particular and insidious and wrong kind of way. And I knew, with no further thought, that I wasn't cut out for any of it.

I guess that's why I had packed up my Kipling duffel bags, teal and seafoam green, high school graduation gifts that had seen me to Europe in the early 2000s, back when people still used traveler's checks. It's why I drove three hours out to an upside-down house in Montauk and rented a room that faced the sea in a place filled with strangers. In Brooklyn, on a thick August morning, you couldn't get a decent plum, my father's favorite, but the farmstands that lined Route 27 and the back roads all the way out to Montauk—Green Thumb Organic Farm in Water Mill or Balsam Farms on the Amagansett line—sold yellow mirabelle plums, and walnut-sized Italian prunes, and shiny black plums with blood-red interiors.

I had been thinking about summer during the gray months of February and March, when the spindly, naked trees brushed up against the windows of my Brooklyn apartment. I had finally left Queens behind after eight years, but my new desolate space only reminded me of one fact: it was the first place that I had ever lived without a father. And so, by day, I took the train into the city, where I worked a traditional job as the head copywriter for Astor Wines & Spirits, and in the evenings I imagined myself taking one last holiday, a summer vacation where I could throw myself back into the kind of restless work that I had done before my father got sick, before I had adult concerns. What if I could go to the ocean for the summer, out toward Montauk and East Hampton, where young people got share houses and spent afternoons lounging in overpriced swimming pools?

On Craigslist, I found leads for a few places, and I spent a few weekends making the long and lonely winter drive out to the Hamptons, looking at rental listings with my rescue dog. There was the cheerful one-bedroom in Springs, owned by a newspaper editor who split his time between the city and the East End. There was, too, the dingy one-bedroom in Montauk that was severely overpriced ($16,000 for the summer, take it or leave it, the agent wants me to know; demand, even in 2013, is at its peak). I was moved by an area outside of Montauk's downtown, off Kettle Hole Road, where the fog doesn't settle unless it's truly bad weather, and where you get a view of the bay and of creeping grape vines from preserved land. When I found a house with a room for rent that felt like a deal, I took it that day.

The job, a sommelier position at Nick & Toni's, came easily, too. My first shift would start one week before Memorial Day Weekend, early enough to get back into the swing of restaurant life before the crush of the holiday. The spirit was ever convivial, the owners were of the mind that the staff was family. On a Saturday night, the parking lot overflowed with Maseratis, Bentleys, G-Wagons, and other luxury vehicles.

Overflow took to North Main Street, where, if you were lucky, you may have borne witness to a fistfight between two white-pant/loafer—bedecked, Ferrari-driving dining enthusiasts. Getting a table was serious business, sure, but so was getting a parking spot.

In the kitchen in my Montauk rental, which I shared with three other thirtysomethings, I began to record memorable celebrity sightings. Paul McCartney, who was a vegetarian and preferred the spicy margarita, served up and with a ring of jalapeño. Nathan Lane, just as gregarious in person as he was on television and in the movies. Alec Baldwin, a regular, prone to ordering off-menu selections and showing up in baggy gray sweatpants with his ever-pregnant yoga-instructor wife. Bill Clinton, now-pescatarian, sometimes the guest of the impossibly cheap Revlon magnate Ron Perelman, who never spent more than $50 on a bottle of rosé. Steven Spielberg, who brought his own terrible Pinot Grigio, produced on his California estate.

The restaurant was run by an octogenarian manager who hated my hair. She wanted it tight, in a chignon. She wanted me buttoned up and reserved, even though she herself violated every rule of the New York State health code, marching in and out of the kitchen in open-toed wedges for hours on end, while I wore sensible clogs, kitchen-approved. My long hair, braided to the side, was too much for her.

"Tie your hair back," she said. I had been hired as the second-in-command sommelier to take the heat off of Julie, since the restaurant was too busy for only one wine professional.

Even as I sold the restaurant's most expensive bottles and commiserated with regulars—even as I won over the monied and
the Hamptons elite—I could not make her like me.

But it didn't matter. I hadn't really come to the Hamptons
to resurrect a life in restaurants. I had come—for real this
time—for a last stab at freedom, to recover from death, to
steal away from one life and into another, to visit another era
in a time capsule. By day, I went for long runs along West
Lake Drive and Old West Lake Drive, past the Crow's Nest,
and sometimes into town, where I'd dip into a store and buy
myself a bottle of water and dump it over my head before
running back home. I had no responsibilities: no ailing father
to care for, no New York City rent. I had sublet my shiny new
Brooklyn apartment so I could playact for a summer, buy
fruits from farmstands, and spend my days falling into naps
on the beach before I had to be at work.

To return to service was to savor the best parts of it: the
chaos, the music, the rhythm. I was thinking about the part
in "4th of July, Asbury Park (Sandy)," the song by Springsteen, about how he didn't think he'd ever get off the Tilt-A-
Whirl. But I had gotten off, I had been off for years, and now
I was choosing to go back on, on purpose, just for a minute,
just for fun. This time, it was going to be different. This time,
it was just going to be a taste.

People in restaurants might tell you that this is impossible, to
come back without staying, to dabble in restaurant culture

without sliding into the restaurant life again. Back in New York, though, I had found something else that felt promising. At Astor, I was being paid to write things—small things. Blurbs about wine. Articles for the website. Experience-based commentary. The previous November, I had sent an unpolished essay off to an editor at the *New York Times*. Six weeks later, while I was out at a bar with friends, that same editor emailed to say that he wanted to run it in a January issue of the newspaper's Modern Love column. Writing in exchange for money still seemed like a fantasy and writing creatively as a career felt out of reach, but the further I moved from restaurants, the more certain I felt that I could do things that were bigger and better than what I had been doing.

So I regarded my time at Nick & Toni's as a playful interlude, a way to heal, a way to process, a way to make peace with an industry that had not always been generous with me but that I still couldn't entirely shake. On any given night, I could scan the reservation system to see what name—and what pseudonym—popped up. What politician, actor, singer, or monied Hamptons non-lebrity would be joining us tonight? Who would be seated in the good section, lining the bamboo screening and facing the pizza ovens, and who would be relegated to "Romper Room" in the back, with the large tables and the echoing cacophony of—can you stand it!?—young children? The room was a brush with fame. To elbow past a Beatle in the dining room was to be reminded of your own mortality. You were only human. You were just a person—an ordinary person just like poor Paul McCartney, legend that he is. He only wants to sit at the end of the bar and drink his spicy margarita in peace. We only want what we want. No more, no less.

The octogenarian kept an iron fist over the book. She was the manager and the maître d', the gate that kept an ordinary citizen from sitting just *anywhere* on a Saturday night at Nick & Toni's. If you wanted a reservation, you had to get through her first. If you were a celebrity, she would know you were coming in. And if you were nobody, you didn't stand a chance.

Big-name tables went to Julie, except for on Sunday and Monday nights, which were the nights when I worked the floor solo. Then, reluctantly, the manager tipped the celebs over to me, almost with derision. She would have preferred to have someone else—anyone else—open their bottles, but I was the designated sommelier on call.

"It's so good to see you again," Spielberg said when he saw me. After the first time, he learned to ask for me by name. I sold him an excellent and expensive Barolo, and he gifted me a bottle of Pinot Grigio in return.

"The tables outside need you," the manager urged, but they only wanted to order cocktails, or wine by the glass. Still, I didn't mind being bossed around by this woman. In the past, restaurant managers and owners and chefs had held sway and authority over me, because I had been malleable. I had wanted to stay and I had too much to lose. But at Nick

& Toni's, I never had both feet in the door. I knew I wasn't hanging around.

"Sure," I told the manager. "Sure, I'll go talk to them." And I did go talk to them, just to pass the time. I had no dreams about a restaurant that was full of a million people who needed my attention. I flowed from room to room with urgency—but more delight than I ever had. She could fire me. I could leave. My house in Montauk was paid through summer. I knew more about wine than almost anyone in the entire restaurant, and the staff seemed to like me well enough. Week after week, the guests came back asking about me, sharing glasses of their own wines, talking about restaurants they thought I should go to, asking my advice: Had I tried the scallop special? What could I say about the La Spinetta rosé? I watched the sunlight paint and weave through bamboo that framed the window on one side of the restaurant, summer like a setting sun.

And it all was like a setting sun, brilliant and pink and orange and memorable, all of the good parts of restaurants that reminded me of being alive and none of the parts that made me want to hide in the walk-in and disappear until the night was over. It was like a bad dream, all of the things that had happened before: Chang's pig-pink face in a hot rage, screaming down at staff on the line; Johnny Iuzzini and his camera, hovering over me, less of a person than a voyeur, a ghost in a room reducing waitstaff to bodies; Jason Wagner and his pink Neruda volumes and stale cigarette breath.

These were characters, when I thought back on them now, people who were not entirely real.

One evening, the manager tried desperately to pull me from the patio, where I was stationed. A big party had come in, and she didn't want me on it, even though she had me out-side, sweating in the summer heat.

"Hannah can take this one," Julie said. She knew who it was. It was Dave. That Dave. Chang. He was rounder than I remembered. I saw him walk in the door, furtively, as if anyone would recognize him. He wasn't television-famous yet. He had gained weight and without whites on looked less intimidating than I remembered. One thing that I did remember: he made no eye contact with staff as he walked through. His handshakes were loose. He was short, and if he had taken up a little less space in the room, you might not have noticed him.

But I did notice him. For a moment, my breath hitched. You never know if someone is going to remember the same things that you remember. He sat outside, at a large table, surrounded by other people who loved to do what he loved to do: eat. Removed from the restaurant, there was, too, the other thing that I remembered, the charming side of him, the way he could win people over. When I came out to offer wine to the table, he looked up with recognition, in the way that people do when they can't quite figure out why they've encountered you in the wrong place and time. It took him a while to put a name to my face, until finally the name came out.

"Hannah," he said.

"That's right," I said.

"What are you doing here?" He assumed, I think, that I was a guest, spending a summer in the Hamptons. And, in a way, that wasn't incorrect. I had come out, at the beginning, at the behest of a friend that I had met working at his restaurant, a friend who kept me in her phone as Momo Hannah. One Memorial Day weekend, she had asked me to drive out and help with the opening of a lakefront restaurant in Montauk, had thrown me a pair of white overalls and a dupe pad and a bag of fresh fruit. "We have no specialty cocktail list and we open in an hour. See what you can do about that," she had told me. When I had fallen in love with the beach scrub and lazy mornings, it had been because of her, but, also, because of him.

"I'm working here. This summer," I said. He wasn't looking at me so much as around, into the garden, at the people, trying to place me contextually in this strange place, the Hamptons. How had I ended up here, in this place of wealth and opportunity, when he had left me back there, abandoned me in the East Village? Well, let bygones be bygones. He offered a glass of wine. It wasn't as if I had forgotten this side of him, exactly. It was the complicated part, the part of Dave that made it hard to hate him, or the part of him that made you wonder which side of him was the real side.

"Do you want to sit?"

I didn't want to sit. I wanted to move on, to see other tables. And I wasn't there to be served, I was there to serve, the constant paradox of being on the other side of the table, never the guest, always the host.

"I'm OK," I said. "Nice to see you."

In some ways, I meant it. It was nice to forget, for a moment, the parts that had soured. He probably wasn't thinking about any of that, not with the rosé flowing on the patio, not with the pink-streaked sunset and the tinny music from the speakers—music he never would have played in his restaurant, music I imagine he hated.

The manager shifted her tune toward the end of the night. "Dave is asking for you," she said. And he was. I had become the point person, somehow. It wasn't like we had anything much to say to one another, and I wasn't a server. But when it came time to pay the check, it was me he wanted to deal with. He slipped a credit card across the table toward me, still tilting his head to the side when it came time to make eye contact. He had never been good at apologies. Was this an attempt at one? Did he even know what he was meant to be apologizing for?

"I just don't want anyone to try to pay the bill," he said.

"No problem," I said.

And although it wasn't really a problem, I knew, somewhere, that it also was, because there was something trans-actional about all of this, because he had cost me a job and accused me of unspeakable things, had indirectly been part of a culture that had crushed me and turned me into a person I hadn't wanted to be. If I hadn't been sure about getting out, I was sure enough about it now, taking that card, holding it in my hand, feeling the weight of it, of the heaviness of service—of serving someone who will never consider you to be their equal, no matter how smart you are, how accomplished, how hardworking. It was all a myth, of working through the pain. Some people held the credit cards. Other people collected them. You had to decide which side of the line you wanted to fall on, if fate allowed. I had to decide which side of the line I wanted to fall on.

I don't want to give Dave Chang too much credit as an arbiter of my destiny. Whether or not he had shown up at that restaurant, a very real literary device—deus ex machina, an English professor would have said—my opinion of restaurant life would no doubt have remained the same. It had run its course. When I had come onto the scene, at 21, I was pink and fresh-skinned, tender and raw, and restaurants had toughened me in both important and insufferable ways. Over a decade later, perched on the precipice of an exit, I wasn't sure if it had been worth it. If your trauma defines you—if it makes you capable of understanding the world differently, or if it gives you something to talk about and write about—is it worth the journey?

But then, to lay waste to a decade without pulling from it

the highs was to forget, with the fuzzy, poor memory of the mistreated, the things that I had, indeed, loved. The food, of course. The thrill of service. If my early days had been marked by the charge of being treated to the best service by other people in the industry, or by the unparalleled buzz of service, my final days in restaurants were marked by the community I found in the Hamptons. Back at BLT Prime, I had been brought to my knees the first time I had a real celebrity sighting. It was Bill Clinton, just a few years off of his presidency. The Secret Service came in first, scoping the restaurant, as is protocol for both current and former presidents. They brought the former president upstairs to a large, round table on the mezzanine. He walked slowly, with charisma.

I charged downstairs, to the employee bathroom, and called both of my parents, speaking in a stage whisper into the phone.

"Bill Clinton is here!"

"Are you calling me from the bathroom?" my father asked.

"Yes!" I shout-talked.

"Go back to work!"

A decade later, when I served Clinton again, this time with Madam Secretary of State—it was just as impressive. They ordered a whole fish and were quiet and kind. The restaurant, so much smaller than BLT, put a spotlight on them. Here was a president, and a prospective one, in a tiny dining room, just ordinary people eating dinner.

As much as I didn't want to be impressed by the constant cavalcade of celebrities who graced the restaurant, I found myself slack-jawed, over and over again. Who wouldn't be addicted to this? Back in the old days, we got high by bumping lines off of toilet seats after service, but I didn't need a line of coke to get high off of restaurants in these final moments, the twilight of my career. It was enough—it was all enough—just to exist in this perfect distillation, a postcard to my former life. Goodbye to all that, but not in the way I had imagined, not in the stomp-your-cigarette-out-with-the-heel-of-your-boot kind of way. It wasn't an angry goodbye, a callous goodbye; it was a kiss. It was a tender reminder of why I had fallen in love in the first place, the blast of heat in the kitchen, where the fryolator was always turning out zucchini chips, and it was the repetition: *behind, behind, behind, corner, corner, corner,* the language of restaurants, the particular and diffuse language shared by servers and service staff. It was the laughter and the feeling of sitting down after a shift and the camaraderie shared among the people who owned the night. Goodbye to all *that.*

I've never been much of a chemical addict, but returning to restaurants after a long hiatus is not far off from what I suspect addicts experience when they return to a familiar drug after a while. The high still feels good, and you forget all of the real and important reasons why you left in the first place. For that first summer, I did forget. I wasn't in my 20s anymore. I was on the appropriate side of the business now, with some years under my belt. I tried to make it home by 1 a.m. and up by 9 a.m. for a run. But after two summers, I realized that you're either a lifer or you aren't, and I had to leave for good.

In the Hamptons, the final day of summer is not Labor Day. It's the day after, the day locals refer to as Tumbleweed Tuesday. That's the day after the tourists leave and the East End of Long Island feels abandoned. You can practically feel the tumbleweeds rolling in, everything returning to its natural state. The schools, in deference to this unofficial holiday, don't begin until the next day, so that restaurant workers and day laborers can enjoy one actual and final day of rest before the fall weather creeps in. Restaurant owners close up shop and host annual parties for staff, who have suffered the indignities of demanding interlopers. It's a send-off to summer, a reminder of the negotiation between local and tourist, the dependency, the need.

That summer, Nick & Toni's held a Tumbleweed Tuesday staff party at Maidstone Beach, in Springs, a community that had been populated by East Hampton fishermen since the 1600s. There, on the beach, in the sharpening dusk, we ate the way the diners we served normally did, a clambake with our feet in the sand, no credit cards exchanged, no bar tabs, no one there to ask us for anything. We were the ones being served.

As I had all of that summer, I was playacting. That night at Maidstone, watching the red-hot sun slip below the horizon on the last official day of the season, I made a mental note. I didn't have to come back. It had been a choice to come back, a choice to be near the ocean, to try to heal in a place that reminded me of my father, and to suck from the marrow of restaurants what I loved about them best. I had done that, and they had given me what I needed. I had made my peace. When no one was looking, I took a flat stone, smoothed it between my index finger and thumb, and cast it into the bay. It skipped once and disappeared into the navy water.

It has now been a decade since my final year in restaurants. Sometimes you have to leave while the party is still going on. Sometimes you have to leave something you love but that isn't good for you. In the end, I left as a whole person. I got out. I walked away.

But Nick & Toni's, and the one restaurant I worked at the summer after it, in 2014, was a final fling, a last gasp. I needed to feel alive again after the death of a parent, to reclaim my youth, but I had already seen too much on the other side. I wasn't really a restaurant person anymore. I was just an imposter trying to get a quick thrill.

* * *

Garlic-Roasted Leg of Lamb with Herb Salsa
Serves 6 to 8 (makes about 1 cup salsa)

LAMB
½ cup (106 grams) olive oil
Cloves from 1 head garlic (about 12), coarsely chopped

1 tablespoon kosher salt

1 teaspoon freshly ground black pepper

1 (6½- to 7-pound) boneless leg of lamb, rolled and tied

SALSA

1 packed cup (25 grams) fresh flat-leaf parsley

½ packed cup (15 grams) fresh mint

6 scallions (white and green parts), trimmed and coarsely
   chopped (or a small handful of chopped fresh chives)

1 large garlic clove, coarsely chopped

1 teaspoon kosher salt, or more as needed

2 tablespoons fresh lemon juice

¼ teaspoon crushed red pepper flakes

½ cup (106 grams) olive oil

For the lamb: Preheat the oven to 400°F. Set an ovenproof wire rack over a rimmed baking sheet lined with aluminum foil.

In a food processor, combine the oil, garlic, salt, and black pepper; pulse to form a smooth paste, stopping to scrape down as needed. (You'll be using the food processor again.)

Spread the garlic paste all over the lamb, then place the meat on the wire rack, fat side up. Roast for 1½ to 2 hours, until the internal temperature registers 135°F on a digital thermometer inserted into the thickest part (for medium-rare). Transfer the lamb to a cutting board, cover loosely with aluminum foil, and let rest for 10 to 20 minutes.

For the salsa: Meanwhile, in a food processor, combine the parsley, mint, scallions, garlic, and salt. Pulse for 30 seconds, or just until incorporated. Add the lemon juice and red pepper flakes; pulse for another 30 seconds. With the motor running, gradually add all the oil to form a smooth, bright-green salsa. You may need to scrape down the sides once or twice and repeat. Taste, and add more salt as needed.

Slice the lamb against the grain into ¼-inch-thick slices, discarding the strings, and arrange the slices on a platter or individual plates. Serve with the herb salsa on the side.

EPILOGUE

For a long time, I kept an apron in the bottom drawer of my desk, as well as a crumber, a silver tray, and a collection of ballpoint pens that were only really suitable for restaurant work. I've finally discarded them. I know, now, that I'll never work in restaurants again, but if you had asked me that five years ago, I probably wouldn't have been able to say that with certainty. I don't look at my time on the floor as time wasted. I had fun, and made friendships, and learned about food and wine in a way that has been instrumental to my work. But I have also been harmed, in deep and lasting ways. Sometimes, even years later, I wake up from a dream that only a former server could have. Imagine a world where it is only you, and where every table in the restaurant needs you, where every order is different, where every detail is one you can't remember.

My friends from restaurants are mostly no longer working

in them. We go to bed at 11 p.m. instead of 5 a.m. We spend our money on home improvement projects and not on tasting menus. And yet, if you get us in the right mood, in the right light, the floodgates will open and our insides will pour out with the trauma that has arrested us for years.

But I do still love restaurants. Like every love affair, it has been a wild and inconsistent ride. Every time I go out to eat and find myself in love—in any small or large way—with a dining experience, this hope returns, a light eternal. I haven't given it up. When I go back to visit, I sometimes have to catch my breath at the way service anticipates my mood or the way I prefer my water.

Not long ago, I dined at a restaurant where I was served a surprise course of squid, something I loathe. When I quietly pawned it off on my husband, I caught the glimmer of recognition later in the meal.

"How did you like the course?"

"I'll be honest," I said. "I don't like squid."

"I know," my host said. "I circled you a few times when you weren't looking." There was no judgment, only empathy. He wanted me to have a great experience, and part of that experience had required his strictest attention to my details. At one point, it had been me on the other end of that telephone cord, strung to a guest's pattern of dining, married to whether or not a dish was too little or too much. Now, the hospitality is mine to enjoy.

I wish I could report that my own sense of peace, messily

achieved after years of trauma, reflects a larger healing within the industry, but restaurants remain broken. So much of the accountability that so many of us have hoped for as we have peeled ourselves back has simply not arrived. We have watched Mario Batali walk out of courtrooms, ready to start anew. We have watched David Chang accept corporate deal after corporate deal. We have watched people like Gabrielle Hamilton shake hands with Ken Friedman, in bargains that feel like they benefit no one but the owners themselves.

The stories of the broken workers have not gotten any smaller or less important. The bones of the forgotten workers pile up. Who tells their stories? A restaurant is a restaurant but for the people who work there, and yet—and still—the industry, I'd argue, has not gotten any less toxic. The only message translated to the people who have lived through the wrath and injustice is that whistleblowing creates a brush-fire that is easily extinguished. The stories are hot until they aren't, and the people who are in power always find a way to retain that power.

I have not given up on fighting for restaurants. This book is only one story. There are others like mine. That I went on to have a home in the suburbs and a husband and two children and dogs and tortoises is part circumstance and part luck, and I am reminded regularly of all the injustice that continues in at-will employment states, where restaurant workers do not have the voice or the power to represent themselves when things go wrong.

Still, I hope that my singular journey—the story of a person who entered an industry ill-equipped to deal with its toxicities and venom and who grew emotionally during her time in it, if not without suffering barbs—is instructive to anyone who wonders if it is possible to come out on the other side as a different version of themselves. Who I am now—a writer, a mother, an advocate for a better restaurant industry—is correlative to what I lived through. Restaurants, even at their worst, made me better. The lesson I took from them was a lesson of borrowing. As I leave these places behind, I borrowed from them what I needed to move on, seeing my scars for what they were. That message, I hope—that trauma is surmountable—lives beyond life in even the most inhospitable of workplaces.

ACKNOWLEDGMENTS

To Debbie Szabo, Kurt Laakso, Jhumpa Lahiri, and Jeff Seglin, four teachers who encouraged my writing long before I had any business calling myself a writer.

To Alice Boone, Jaime Sneider, Adam Kushner, and Dan Laidman, all of whom had the misfortune of editing me at the *Columbia Spectator*, the first place where I found a community of like-minded colleagues. To Artie Harris, I think of you often.

To Meghan Kortmann, Georgie Menu, Joe Shaw, Paul Brady, Mel Hansche, Erin DeJesus, Matt Buchanan, Dan Jones, and all the other editors who have been so instrumental in shaping my career. No one writes in a vacuum, and I am indebted to all of you for granting me opportunities when I was a young writer, for allowing me to tell true and personal stories, and for celebrating my admittedly unique voice.

To my indispensable recipe tester, Bonnie Benwick, who went above and beyond to make sure that the food content included herein was delicious, accurately written, and deserving of posterity.

To the people who taught me about food, wine, and service along the way: thank you. We had some good times! I wish I could list every single influence who helped shape the greatest parts of my restaurant career, from the porters to the chefs, but that's a long list. But I'd like to acknowledge some of these people, not all of whom are still with us: Tia Keenan, Hristo Zisovski, Celine Valensi, Marc Forgione, Thierry Sighel, Bill Nichelmann, Colin Campbell, John Coyle, Jessica Svensson, Frank Nobiletti, Melissa Termyna, and Chris Leahy.

To my agents, Rick Richter and Caroline Marsiglia, who have suffered the indignities of my punctuality, constant emails, and check-ins, and who have never stopped believing in my zany projects.

To my incredible and fierce book editor, Vivian Lee, a cease-less advocate for all her writers, and for all people (and who still likes me, somehow, even though she follows me on Instagram).

To the Applesauce Club, who have listened to far more of their share of grievances, both writing-related and not. To Jessika, for 35-ish years of friendship, most of which has been spent not fighting. To Helen, my most treasured inheritance from my Momo Trauma.™ To Auld Gay, because he requested this particular moniker. To Char Drucks, a great listener. To Hannah Howard, an excellent partner.

And to all my other friends, from Newburyport (you all know who you are, *bubba we, yeat,* and my deepest apologies for grouping you together in one shameful parenthetical), to Kippewa, FCI, San Francisco, the Hamptons, Columbia and Barnard, Brooklyn, Manhattan, and beyond, who have championed this project and others, and who continue to amaze me with their talents, their kindness, and their support.

To Pickle, who may not be around by the time this is published, but who taught me a lot of what I needed to know about love.

To my father, Neil, who really would have loved every minute of this. Regrets, I've had a few, but one is that I couldn't change the trajectory of time and make this happen while you were still alive.

To my mother, Judith; my mother-in-kind, Rima; to my sisters, Emily, Julia, and Meagan; and to my brother, Casey, with no further explanation.

To my children, Nathaniel and Miles, who are the light of my life, and whom I hope grasp that it is such a privilege to be able to do what you love for a living. I hope that you, too, find your passion and get to live it out fully.

To my husband, Dan, who didn't blink when I said I was quitting my job to write full-time, and who also didn't blink when I made no money that first year. I'm glad it worked out!

To the people of Gaza, who cannot, at the time of this writing, pen books with such facility, because there are no universities left, because 60 percent of Gaza's educational facilities have been destroyed with the help of American dollars, because we have taken even the spaces where Gazans have sought refuge, because this is the world we have left in the wake of terrible and unjustifiable genocide. Yes, genocide.

This book is yours, too.

ABOUT THE AUTHOR

Hannah Selinger is a James Beard Award–nominated writer living in Boxford, Massachusetts, with her husband, two sons, two dogs, and one Russian tortoise. Her work has appeared in the *New York Times Magazine, Food & Wine, Travel + Leisure,* the *Wall Street Journal,* the *New York Times,* the *Washington Post,* the *Boston Globe,* and elsewhere, and has been anthologized in *The Best American Food Writing* series. This is her first book.